The Growth and Influence of Islam

IN THE NATIONS OF ASIA AND CENTRAL ASIA

Muslims in Russia

The Growth and Influence of Islam
IN THE NATIONS OF ASIA AND CENTRAL ASIA

Afghanistan

Azerbaijan

Bangladesh

Indonesia

Islam in Asia: Facts and Figures

Islamism and Terrorist Groups in Asia

Kazakhstan

The Kurds

Kyrgyzstan

Malaysia

Muslims in China

Muslims in India

Muslims in Russia

Pakistan

Tajikistan

Turkmenistan

Uzbekistan

The Growth and Influence of Islam

IN THE NATIONS OF ASIA AND CENTRAL ASIA

Muslims in Russia

Uli Schamiloglu

Mason Crest Publishers
Philadelphia

Dedication: For Yasmin & Bulat

Produced by OTTN Publishing, Stockton, New Jersey

Mason Crest Publishers
370 Reed Road
Broomall, PA 19008
www.masoncrest.com

First printing

1 3 5 7 9 8 6 4 2

Library of Congress Cataloging-in-Publication Data

Schamiloglu, Uli.
  Muslims in Russia / Uli Schamiloglu.
     p. cm. — (Growth and influence of Islam in the nations of Asia and Central Asia)
  Includes bibliographical references and index.
  ISBN-13: 978-1-59084-884-5
  ISBN-10: 1-59084-884-5
 1. Muslims—Russia—History. 2. Muslims—Soviet Union--History. 3.
Muslims—Russia (Federation)—History. I. Title. II. Series.
  DK34.M8S33 2006
  947'.088'297—dc22
                                        2005023336

The Growth and Influence of Islam
In the Nations of Asia and Central Asia

Table of Contents

Introduction..7
  Harvey Sicherman, the Foreign Policy Research Institute

Overview 13

The Land & Political-Territorial Distribution 23

Muslims in Russia in the Medieval Period 31

From the Russian Conquest to the 19th Century...49

Islamic Modernism in the Russian Empire 65

Islam in the USSR...77

Islam in the Russian Federation...........................95

Diversity Among Russia's Muslims 115

Conclusion: The Future of Islam in Russia 129

Glossary 134

Selected Bibliography 136

Internet Resources..142

Index 144

Muslim citizens of the USSR pray in a mosque, circa 1990.

Dr. Harvey Sicherman, president and director of the Foreign Policy Research Institute, is the author of such books as *America the Vulnerable: Our Military Problems and How to Fix Them* **(2002) and** *Palestinian Autonomy, Self-Government and Peace* **(1993).**

Introduction

by Dr. Harvey Sicherman

A merica's triumph in the Cold War promised a new burst of peace and prosperity. Indeed, the decade between the demise of the Soviet Union and the destruction of September 11, 2001, proved deceptively hopeful. Today, of course, we are more fully aware—to our sorrow—of the dangers and troubles no longer just below the surface.

The Muslim identities of most of the terrorists at war with the United States have also provoked great interest in Islam as well as the role of religion in politics. It is crucial for Americans not to assume that Osama bin Laden's ideas are identical to those of most Muslims or, for that matter, that most Muslims are Arabs. A truly world religion, Islam claims hundreds of millions of adherents, from every ethnic group scattered across the globe. This book series covers the growth and influence of Muslims in Asia and Central Asia.

A glance at the map establishes the extraordinary coverage of our authors. Every climate and terrain may be found, along with every form of human society, from the nomadic groups of the Central Asian steppes to highly sophisticated cities such as Singapore, New Delhi, and Shanghai. The economies of the nations examined in this series are likewise highly diverse. In some, barter systems are still used; others incorporate modern stock markets. In some of the countries, large oil reserves hold out the prospect of prosperity. Other countries, such as India and China, have progressed by moving from a government-controlled to a more market-based economic system. Still other countries have built wealth on service and shipping.

Central Asia and Asia is a heavily armed and turbulent area. Three of its states (China, India, and Pakistan) are nuclear powers, and one (Kazakhstan) only recently rid itself of nuclear weapons. But it is also a place where the horse and mule remain indispensable instruments of war. All of the region's states have an extensive history of conflict, domestic and international, old and new. Afghanistan, for example, has known little but invasion and civil war over the past two decades.

Governments include dictatorships, democracies, and hybrids without a name; centralized and decentralized administrations; and older patterns of tribal and clan associations. The region is a veritable encyclopedia of political expression.

Although such variety defies easy generalities, it is still possible to make several observations. First, the geopolitics of Central Asia and Asia reflect the impact of empires and the struggles of post-imperial independence. Central Asia, a historic corridor for traders and soldiers, was the scene of Russian expansion well into Soviet times. While Kazakhstan's leaders participated in the historic meeting of December 25, 1991, that dissolved the Soviet Union, the rest of the region's newly independent republics hardly expected it. They have found it difficult to grapple with a sometimes tenuous independence, buffeted by a strong residual Russian influence, the absence of settled institutions, the temptation of newly valuable natural resources, and mixed populations lacking a solid national identity. The shards of the Soviet Union have often been sharp—witness the Russian war in Chechnya—and sometimes fatal for those ambitious to grasp them.

Moving further east, one encounters an older devolution, that of the half-century since the British Raj dissolved into India and Pakistan (the latter giving violent birth to Bangladesh in 1971). Only recently, partly under the impact of the war on terrorism, have these nuclear-armed neighbors and adversaries found it possible to renew attempts at reconciliation. Still further east, Malaysia shares a British experience, but Indonesia has been influenced by its Dutch heritage. Even China defines its own borders along the lines of the Qing empire (the last pre-republican dynasty) at its most expansionist (including Tibet and Taiwan). These imperial histories lie heavily upon the politics of the region.

A second aspect worth noting is the variety of economic experimentation afoot in the area. State-dominated economic strategies, still in the ascendant, are separating government from the actual running of commerce and industry. "Privatization," however, is frequently a byword for crony capitalism and corruption. Yet in dynamic economies such as that of China, as well as an increasingly productive India, hundreds of millions of people have dramatically improved both their standard of living and their hope for the future. All of them aspire to benefit from international trade. Competitive advantages, such as low-cost labor (in some cases trained in high technology) and valuable natural resources (oil, gas, and minerals), promise much. This is indeed a revolution of rising expectations, some of which are being satisfied.

Yet more than corruption threatens this progress. Population increase, even though moderating, still overwhelms educational and employment opportunities. Many countries are marked by extremes of wealth and poverty, especially between rural and urban areas. Dangerous jealousies threaten ethnic groups (such as anti-Chinese violence in Indonesia). Hopelessly overburdened public services portend turmoil. Public health, never adequate, is harmed further by environmental damage to critical resources (such as the Aral Sea). By and large, Central Asian and Asian countries are living well beyond their infrastructures.

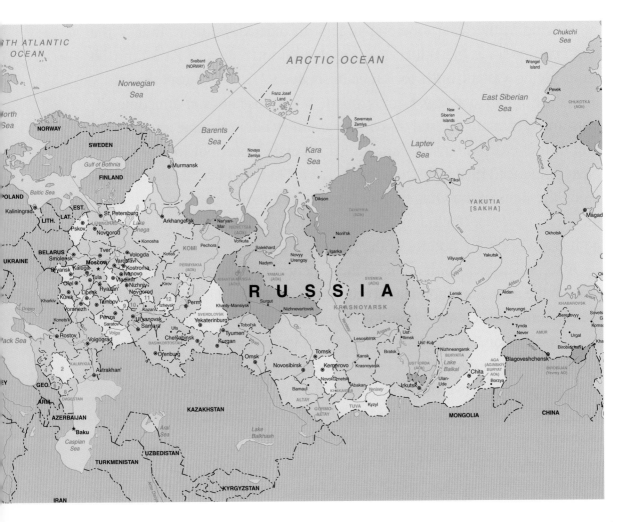

Third and finally, Islam has deeply affected the states and peoples of the region. Indonesia is the largest Muslim state in the world, and India hosts the second-largest Muslim population. Islam is not only the official religion of many states, it is the very reason for Pakistan's existence. But Islamic practices and groups vary: the well-known Sunni and Shiite groups are joined by energetic Salafi (Wahabi) and Sufi movements. Over the last 20 years especially, South and Central Asia have become battle-grounds for competing Shiite (Iranian) and Wahabi (Saudi) doctrines, well financed from abroad and aggressively antagonistic toward non-Muslims and each other. Resistance to the Soviet invasion of Afghanistan brought these groups battle-tested warriors and organizers. The war on terrorism has exposed just how far-reaching and active the new advocates of holy war (jihad) can be. Indonesia, in particular, is the scene of rivalry between an older, tolerant Islam and the jihadists. But Pakistan also faces an Islamic identity crisis. And India, wracked by sectarian strife, must hold together its democratic framework despite Muslim and Hindu extremists. This newly significant struggle within Islam, superimposed on an older Muslim history, will shape political and economic destinies throughout the region and beyond. Hence, the focus of our series.

We hope that these books will enlighten both teacher and student about a critical subject in a critical area of the world. Central Asia and Asia would be important in their own right to Americans; arguably, after 9/11, they became vital to our national security. And the enduring impact of Islam is a crucial factor we must understand. We at the Foreign Policy Research Institute hope these books will illuminate both the facts and the prospects.

A Muslim reads from a religious book in Arabic script, in front of a Russian mosque. Today, more than 12.5 million Muslims live in the Russian Federation.

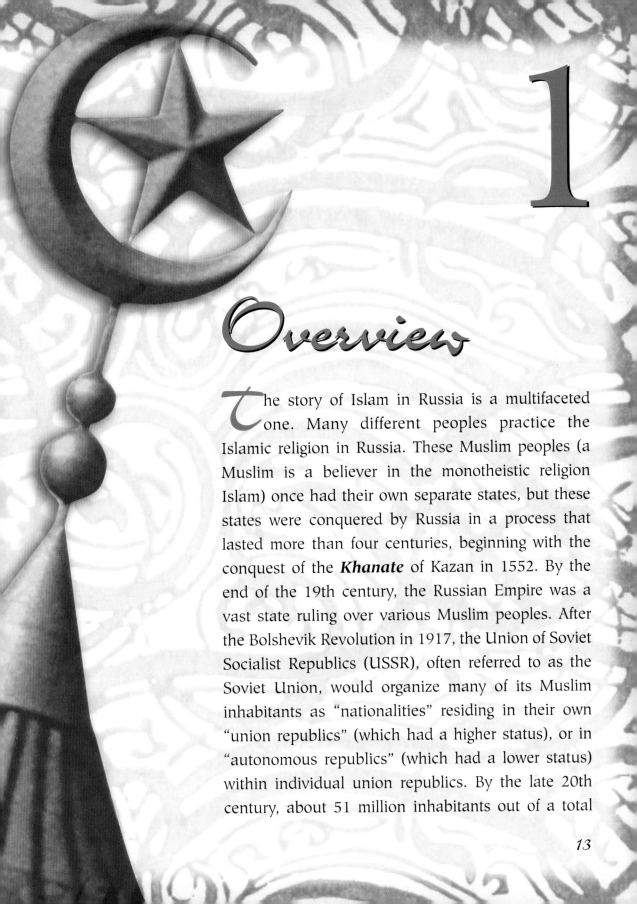

1

Overview

$\mathcal{T}$he story of Islam in Russia is a multifaceted one. Many different peoples practice the Islamic religion in Russia. These Muslim peoples (a Muslim is a believer in the monotheistic religion Islam) once had their own separate states, but these states were conquered by Russia in a process that lasted more than four centuries, beginning with the conquest of the **Khanate** of Kazan in 1552. By the end of the 19th century, the Russian Empire was a vast state ruling over various Muslim peoples. After the Bolshevik Revolution in 1917, the Union of Soviet Socialist Republics (USSR), often referred to as the Soviet Union, would organize many of its Muslim inhabitants as "nationalities" residing in their own "union republics" (which had a higher status), or in "autonomous republics" (which had a lower status) within individual union republics. By the late 20th century, about 51 million inhabitants out of a total

Soviet population of 286,717,000 (1989 census) belonged to traditionally Muslim ethnic groups.

Since the collapse of the USSR in 1991, the 15 former union republics have become 15 independent states. Of these, Russia (officially the "Russian Federation") is the largest, containing about three-fifths of the population of the former Soviet Union. Today Russia is home to many different Muslim peoples, who make up about 8.6 percent of its population. According to the 2002 census, 12,491,000 inhabitants out of the total Russian Federation population of 145,164,000 belong to traditionally Muslim ethnic groups. However, some unofficial estimates put the number of Muslims in Russia at closer to 20 million, which would mean that Muslims constitute more than 13 percent of the population. (This will be discussed in detail in Chapter 8.) In any case, Islam continues to be a dynamic religious, cultural, and political force in Russia today.

This book will examine:
- where the Muslims of Russia live
- the history of Islam as a religion and civilization in Russia
- the Russian state's policies toward its Muslims
- the diverse modern ethnic groups comprising the Muslim population of Russia
- the various political, social, cultural, and economic problems confronting the Muslims of Russia today.

Before proceeding, we should briefly review the major features of Islam, a religion that today claims more than a billion adherents worldwide.

What Is Islam?

Islam is a monotheistic religion founded in Arabia in the early seventh century C.E. Muslims believe that the word of God (*Allah,* in Arabic) was revealed to the prophet Muhammad (ca. 570–632) and was later preserved in the Qur'an (or Koran), which was committed to writing by the Companions of the Prophet soon after his death. The Qur'an, which is in the Arabic language, is Muslims' scripture or Holy Book. It is also considered the most beautiful literary work in the Arabic language.

Like Judaism and Christianity, the world's other major monotheistic faiths, Islam traces its descent through the patriarch Abraham. In addition to Abraham, Muslims recognize as prophets all the major figures of the Judeo-Christian tradition, from Adam down to Jesus Christ. Muhammad is considered the last of God's prophets and is therefore called the "seal of the prophets."

There are five fundamental principles or "pillars of faith" in Islam:

1. The first pillar of faith is the unity of God. In order to become a Muslim, all one has to do is recite in Arabic the following formula: "There is no God but Allah and Muhammad is his Messenger."

2. The second pillar is prayer five times a day (before dawn, at noon, in the afternoon, after sunset, and in the evening). Prayers, which are preceded by ritual ablutions, are conducted in Arabic, but sermons are conducted in the local language.

3. The third pillar is fasting from dawn to dusk during the month of Ramadan (Ramazan in local languages in Russia).

4. The fourth pillar is almsgiving. Each year Muslims are required to give 1/40 (or 2.5 percent) of their total wealth (not income!) as alms to the poor.

5. The fifth pillar is **hajj**, or pilgrimage to the holy city of Mecca (in Saudi Arabia). Muslims who are free of debt are obligated to undertake this journey once in their lifetime. All Muslims on the pilgrimage are dressed alike in pure white

Muslims bow in prayer while circled around the Kaaba during the hajj, a ritual pilgrimage to the city of Mecca in Saudi Arabia. Muslims consider the Kaaba, an ancient square stone building draped in black, to be the holiest place in the world. Participation in the hajj is one of the five major precepts, or pillars, of Islam.

cloth and are obligated to remain in a state of purity and forgo bloodshed.

While all Sunni Muslims (who constitute the majority of followers of Islam worldwide) agree on the above five "pillars of faith," there is tremendous doctrinal diversity in the Sunni Muslim world. Although the Qur'an and the sayings (Hadith) attributed to the prophet Muhammad form the original basis of Islamic law (**Sharia**), over time four separate traditions of jurisprudence, known as legal schools (Arabic *madhhab*; *mazhab* in local languages in Russia), also developed: Hanafi, Maliki, Shafii, and Hanbali. The Muslims of Russia belong mostly to the Hanafi school, which is also dominant in certain Arab countries of the Middle East, including Syria and Iraq, as well as in South Asia (Pakistan, India). The Hanbali school is the official legal school in Saudi Arabia; the Maliki school is dominant in North Africa; and the Shafii school is popular in Egypt, among the Kurds of the Middle East, and in Southeast Asia.

The most important division in the Muslim world is the schism between the majority Sunnis (who adhere to Islam's "orthodox" tradition) and the minority Shiites (who constitute about 15 percent of all Muslims).

The Sunni-Shia schism grew out of a controversy over who should become leader of the Muslim community (*umma*) following Muhammad's death. One group, who would become the Sunnis, believed that the Prophet's successor as both leader in prayer (**imam**) and political leader (caliph) should be chosen from among the Muslim community's pious men. Another group, who would become known as the Shiites, insisted that succession should be hereditary; as Muhammad had no sons who survived to adulthood, they believed his closest male relative, his cousin and son-in-law Ali, should be his successor. The Sunni view prevailed, however, and three men—Abu Bakr, Umar, and Uthman—were chosen as caliphs before Ali was finally picked in 656.

From this very early period in Islamic history, Shiites developed a theological and legal tradition entirely different from the Sunni tradition. This tradition stresses the concept of the "infallible Imam" as the political and religious leader of the Shiites. Shiites show a deep veneration for Ali and his martyred son Husayn (including the celebration of their martyrdom on the 10th of Muharram according to the Islamic calendar). Sunni Muslims find this to be anti-Islamic. Shiites live mostly in Azerbaijan, Iran, Iraq, the Persian Gulf region, and South Asia.

Ethnic Groups

So who are the Muslims of Russia anyway? Historically, most of the Muslims of the Russian Empire lived in three distinct regions: the Middle Volga region, the Caucasus, and Central Asia. Today, the Muslims of the South Caucasus live in the state of Azerbaijan. The Muslims of Central Asia live in five independent states: Kazakhstan, Turkmenistan, Uzbekistan, Tajikistan, and Kyrgyzstan. The Muslims of the North Caucasus and the Middle Volga region form a part of the Russian Federation. (In Ukraine there is a significant Muslim minority in the Crimea, the historic home of the Crimean Tatars.)

The Muslims of the Middle Volga region are largely Kazan Tatars (also known as Volga Tatars) and Bashkirs (Bashqort), who are two closely related Turkic peoples. (The Kazan Tatar and Bashkir languages belong to the same subgroup of the Kipchak dialect group of the Turkic languages.) Tatars and Bashkirs live mostly in the adjoining republics of Tatarstan and Bashqortostan, with additional Tatar minorities in the republics of Udmurtia, Mari El, and Chuvashia, and in the regions of the cities of Penza, Simbirsk (Ul'yanovsk), and Samara. Significant numbers of Kazan

These Tatar dancers from the Kazan region of Russia are wearing traditional dress.

Tatars also live in major cities outside these regions, especially in Moscow and St. Petersburg, along the lower course of the Volga River (Saratov, Astrakhan), in Orenburg, and in Siberia (Perm, Yekaterinaburg, Chelyabinsk, Tyumen, and other cities). In the southern part of this same region there are also Kazakhs (another Muslim Turkic people whose language also belongs to the Kipchak group of the Turkic languages), especially around the city of Saratov near the border with Kazakhstan.

The other traditional concentration of Muslims is the North Caucasus between the Black Sea and the Caspian Sea. While a few of these mountain peoples speak a Turkic language (Karachays, Balkars, Kumyks, and Nogays) or an Iranian language very distantly related to English (the Ossetians, who are Christians), most of them speak a "Caucasian" language. Caucasian languages are divided into several groups:

1. Speakers of South Caucasian languages (or "Kartvelian" languages, including Georgian) are mostly non-Muslims. The one exception is the Adjarians, who are Muslim Georgians and live outside of present-day Russia.

2. In the Russian Federation today speakers of Northeast and Northwest Caucasian languages are Muslims. The Northeast Caucasian (Nakh-Dagestanian) languages include the Vaynakh group (Chechen, Ingush) and the Avaro-Andi-Tsez group (Avar, Dargin, Lezgi, Lak, Tabarasan, Rutul, Agul, Tsakhur). The Northwest Caucasian languages include Circassian (including Kabarda in the east and Adyge in the west), Abaza, and Abkhaz.

In the 1990s speakers of Northeast and Northwest Caucasian languages lived mostly in Adygeya, Chechnya, Dagestan, Ingushetia, Kabardino-Balkaria, Karachayevo-Cherkessia, and North Osetia (also spelled Ossetia in English). More recently there has been official talk of reorganizing the republics of the North Caucasus because of ethnic conflict spreading as a result of the two wars in Chechnya.

We will discuss the ethnic groups to which the Muslims of Russia belong in greater detail in Chapter 8.

Islam in Russia: Today and the Future

Since the collapse of the USSR in 1991, the Muslims of Russia have been at the center of great questions facing the Russian Federation as it maps out its future:

- Is Russia to be a multi-confessional state, with Islam as one of the recognized and supported faiths, or will it be a state in which

St. Basil's Cathedral in Moscow, built to honor the conquest of the Khanate of Kazan, is one of Russia's most famous landmarks. Many Russians are members of the Russian Orthodox Church, and although Islam is currently recognized by the state, along with other religions, some Orthodox Christians are trying to make their faith the official religion of Russia.

Orthodox Christianity is favored as the state religion? (Currently Islam has a special status as one of the traditional religions of Russia, but some supporters of the Orthodox Church are trying to promote that religion over other religions in Russia.)

• Is Russia to be a multi-ethnic state, or will it promote Russian language and culture at the expense of minority languages and cultures, including those of Muslim minorities?

• Will Russia continue to be a federal state, recognizing the rights granted Muslim and non-Muslim ethnic republics in the Soviet period, or will it seek to eliminate the separate national republics? (And if it eliminates those republics, will it provide instead national cultural autonomy without national republics?)

• Will Russia make a serious effort to end ethnic conflict in places where there is currently bloody war (especially Chechnya)?

These are all important questions the Russian Federation must face as it charts its future. While it seems unlikely, in the end Russia may decide to encourage its Muslim ethnic minorities to become linguistically and culturally Russian, and perhaps even to convert to Orthodox Christianity (echoing policies of earlier centuries). It is doubtful, however, that a policy of forced religious conversion can be successful in this day and age.

There is yet another emerging phenomenon that deserves mention, namely that of "Russian Islam." Many ethnic Russians of Orthodox Christian background are converting to Islam, which is a rapidly growing religion in Russia. Even if Russia's Muslim minorities were to assimilate to Russian culture as "Russian Muslims," it would only contribute to the growth of a new and larger community of Russian Muslims, parallel to the growing phenomenon of Euro-Islam in Western Europe.

Oil drilling equipment rises above the harsh terrain of Nefteyugansk in western Siberia. Russia, which stretches across the continent of Asia, is the world's largest country in terms of total land area.

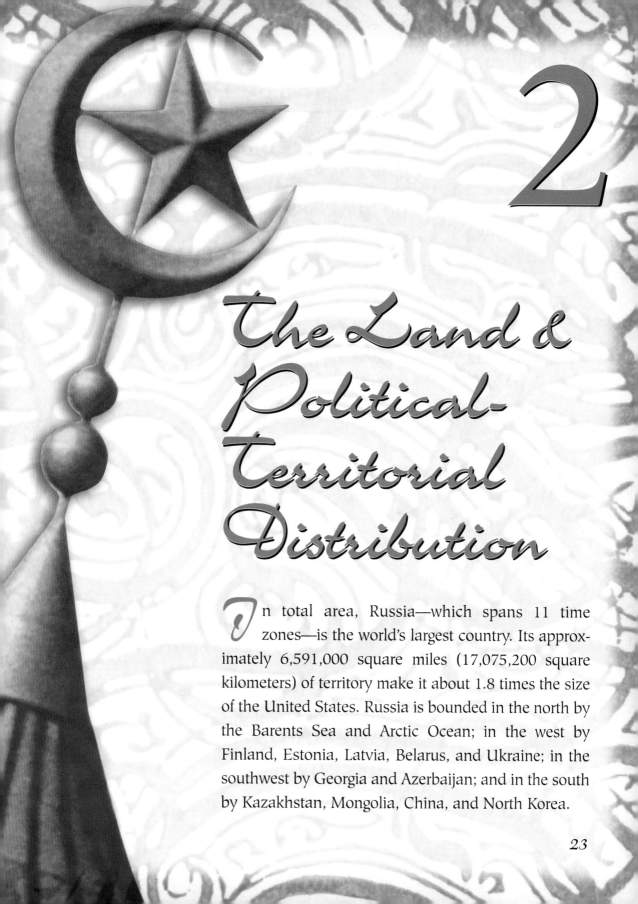

2

The Land & Political-Territorial Distribution

𝓘n total area, Russia—which spans 11 time zones—is the world's largest country. Its approximately 6,591,000 square miles (17,075,200 square kilometers) of territory make it about 1.8 times the size of the United States. Russia is bounded in the north by the Barents Sea and Arctic Ocean; in the west by Finland, Estonia, Latvia, Belarus, and Ukraine; in the southwest by Georgia and Azerbaijan; and in the south by Kazakhstan, Mongolia, China, and North Korea.

23

Traditional populations in the Russian Empire lived under a wide variety of conditions. To the far south, in Central Asia, the arid terrain around the harsh Karakum and Kyzylkum deserts was home to Turkmen nomads who relied on camels for transportation and also kept herds of horses and sheep. The neighboring dry, hot regions had an oasis culture populated by Uzbeks and Tajiks who relied on water from wells and rivers such as the Amu Darya and Syr Darya to irrigate their crops. This area has always been known for its bounty of crops that prefer a long, hot growing season, including nuts, apricots, plums, grapes, and melons. Areas with higher elevations, such as the Fergana Valley, were centers of rich agricultural production. The high mountainous regions ringing the southern parts of Central Asia were inhabited by Kyrgyz and Tajik nomads who would take their sheep and yaks to alpine pastures in the summer and camp in lower-altitude valleys during the winter.

To the west, between the Black Sea and the Caspian Sea, is the mountainous region known as the Caucasus. The high rugged mountains divide this region into distinct northern and southern zones with a wide range of microclimates suitable for a wide range of crops. Animal husbandry is practiced in the grasslands of the North Caucasus as well as in the higher altitudes of the mountain ranges. The southern zone has diverse microclimates permitting the cultivation of a wide range of crops. To the west, jutting into the Black Sea, is the Crimea. This peninsula is divided into a northern zone, which is dry grassland, and a richly productive southern coastline that is reminiscent of the California coastline.

The next zone to the north is the largely treeless grassland known as the steppe. It stretches west across most of the territory of present-day Kazakhstan, the territory north of the Caspian Sea, the North Caucasus headland, and the territory north of the Black Sea. (The steppe's easternmost extension is in Mongolia and Manchuria; its westernmost extension is the Great Hungarian Plain.) Throughout most of history, pastoral

Russia has a rich cultural history. The Hermitage, a famous museum in St. Petersburg, contains one of the world's finest art collections.

nomads inhabited the steppe. They spent the winter in the southern pastures and traveled to northern pastures for the summer, when the southern grasslands often turned to semi-desert. The 19th and 20th centuries saw major colonization of the northern steppe zone in present-day Kazakhstan by Slavic and German agriculturalists.

Northeast of this region is the vast territory of Siberia, famous in the south for its evergreen forests and in the north for its tundra. While the areas of northeastern Siberia were traditionally inhabited by native reindeer-breeders such as the Turkic-speaking Yakut, in southern Siberia there were numerous cities that were an extension of the northern steppe zone.

The Volga River, a major artery that flows some 2,290 miles (3,690 km) before emptying into the Caspian Sea, connected the Slavic peoples to the north with the peoples of the Middle and Lower Volga regions. The Middle Volga region, located to the north of the steppe zone, stretches in a cone-like shape toward the core Slavic territories of northwest Russia. This is a region with a moderate summer climate and long, harsh winters. Sufficient rainfall enabled the region's traditional inhabitants to practice agriculture without the irrigation necessary for successful harvests in the south. Grains such as wheat, rye, and oats were grown; fodder sustained the animals during the long winter. The local populations also lived on fish, vegetables, legumes, fruits (apples, cherries), berries, honey, dairy products, sheep, and other agricultural products typical of a more northerly climate.

The Muslims of the Russian Empire traditionally lived in a number of distinct regions: the Crimea, the North Caucasus region, the South Caucasus region (also known as the Transcaucasus), the Middle Volga region (extending into the Ural Mountain region), Central Asia, the steppe region extending north of Central Asia and the Caucasus, and, in more recent centuries, Siberia. In the Russian Federation today the greatest concentrations of Muslims are in the North Caucasus, the Middle Volga region, western Siberia, cities along the Volga River such as Saratov and Astrakhan, and—surprisingly—Moscow and St. Petersburg.

What Is Russia?

Before going any further, we also need to define what we mean by "Russia" in this work. The Russian Federation, as it is officially known, is but one of 15 successor states to the USSR. Its modern boundaries are largely arbitrary products of the 20th century, as are the boundaries of the other 14 successor states to the USSR (Armenia, Azerbaijan, Belarus, Estonia, Georgia, Kazakhstan, Kyrgyzstan, Latvia, Lithuania, Moldova, Tajikistan, Turkmenistan, Ukraine, and Uzbekistan).

The rapid transformation of the principality of Muscovy (Moscow) into an empire began in 1552, the year of Russia's first conquest of a

Russian and Kazakh fishermen use a net to catch sturgeon in the Volga River near Astrakhan.

neighboring state, the Muslim Khanate of Kazan in the Middle Volga region. By 1689 the Russian Empire claimed almost all the territory of Central Eurasia (a recent term generally denoting the territories between Russia, the Middle East, South Asia, and China inhabited by Muslim or Turkic, Iranian, and other non-Slavic peoples) as far as the Pacific Ocean. By the late 19th century the Russian Empire had completed its bloody conquest of Central Asia and the Caucasus. In other words, much of the territory of the Russian Empire had already been claimed in the 17th century, and all of the territory that would later form a part of the USSR had been conquered by the late 19th century.

Although the way in which the Russian state governed the different parts of its vast empire varied, in many important ways the Muslims of this huge territory formed a single community at different points in time. For example, one can speak of a larger Islamic civilization in this territory during the Mongol period (13th to 14th centuries). One can also speak of a single "imagined community" of Muslim Turks in the Russian Empire in the late 19th to early 20th centuries. Throughout the history of the Russian Empire from the 16th century to the early 20th century, and even in the Soviet period (1917–1991), it is difficult—if not impossible—to speak only of those Muslims living on the territory of the present-day Russian Federation.

This territory would continue as a single state during the time of the USSR, which reconfigured its ethnic map with the recognition—some would say creation—of new "nationalities." By the 1930s, these new nationalities would be the basis of new union republics and, within certain union republics (especially the Russian Federation, known by the abbreviation "RSFSR"), of new autonomous republics. The illogical boundaries of these new republics did not always follow earlier boundaries separating ethnic and linguistic groups. Nevertheless, there was a state ideology of "friendship of peoples" throughout the Soviet period, and as long as the USSR was really run as a centralized state from Moscow, ethnic tensions were under control. Sometimes the "friendship of peoples" was proven to be just for show: in 1944, for example, the Soviet leader Joseph Stalin ordered the deportation to Central Asia of Muslim Chechens, Ingush, Karachays, and other peoples from the Caucasus, as well as the Crimean Tatars from the Crimea (along with the non-Muslim Volga Germans). Later, during the 1980s, republics such as Tatarstan sought greater autonomy. Once the USSR imploded in 1991, the door was opened for new ethnic conflicts. While

Tatarstan was able to negotiate successfully for greater autonomy, the Chechen bid for independence has been crushed by two bloody wars.

This work focuses on the territory of the Russian Federation today, but at times it cannot help but refer to the Muslims of the Russian Empire and the USSR as a whole. Some statements that appear may be applicable to Muslims in what is today Azerbaijan, Turkmenistan, Kazakhstan, Kyrgyzstan, Uzbekistan, Tajikistan, and other independent states, even if they are not the focus of this work. While many peoples of the former Soviet Union now have their own states, in Russia today there are significant minorities of all these peoples—which only underscores how difficult it is to speak of the Muslims of the territory of the Russian Federation as something totally separate from the Muslims of the other "newly independent" states.

Political Organization of Russia

Today the Russian Federation continues a system of political organization that it inherited from the USSR. Currently it is divided into 49 provinces (*oblast'*), 21 republics (*respublika*), 10 autonomous regions (*avtonomnyi okrug*), 6 districts (*kray*), 2 federal cities (*gorod*), and 1 autonomous province (*avtonomnaya oblast'*). The republics and many of the lower-level administrative units are based on nationality, a Soviet-era term for ethnic group that has been transformed into a modern national-territorial political unit. Most of these nationalities did not have a national-territorial identity before the establishment of such national political units during the Soviet period.

The most important nationality-based political units are the 21 republics. Those representing traditionally Muslim ethnic groups or nationalities are Adygeya, Bashqortostan, Chechnya, Dagestan, Ingushetia, Kabardino-Balkaria, Karachayevo-Cherkessia, and Tatarstan.

Ancient Turkic nomads carved this figure into a stela, or standing stone, on the Eurasian steppe. The Turkic peoples gradually migrated throughout Asia, and many embraced Islam between the 8th and 11th centuries A.D.

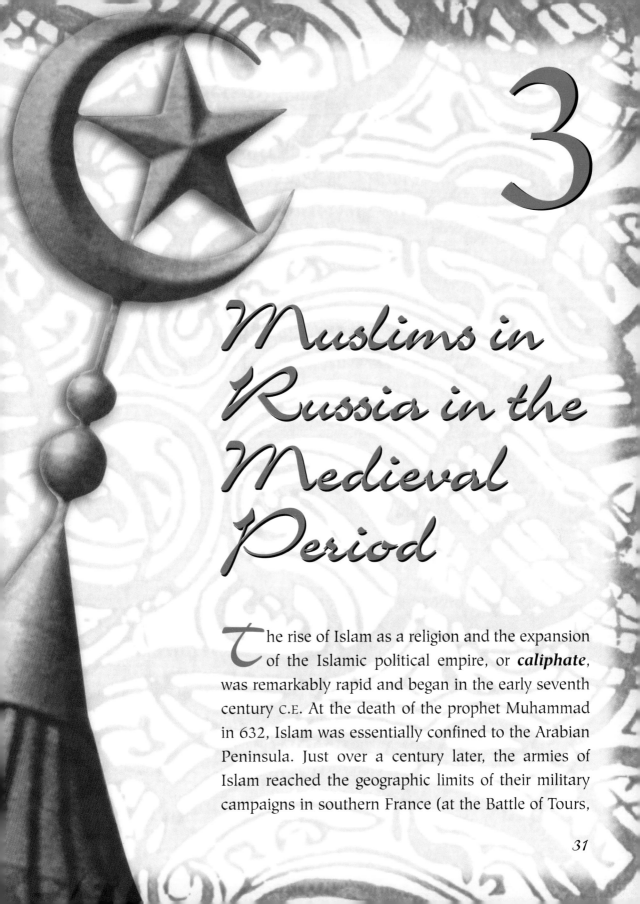

3

Muslims in Russia in the Medieval Period

The rise of Islam as a religion and the expansion of the Islamic political empire, or **caliphate**, was remarkably rapid and began in the early seventh century C.E. At the death of the prophet Muhammad in 632, Islam was essentially confined to the Arabian Peninsula. Just over a century later, the armies of Islam reached the geographic limits of their military campaigns in southern France (at the Battle of Tours,

732) and Central Asia (at the Battle of Talas, 751). It is during the second half of this initial period of expansion of the caliphate—specifically in the early eighth century—that we can first speak of Islam's expansion onto the territories of what much later would become the Russian Empire (and in the 20th century, the USSR).

To what can we attribute the rapid expansion of the Islamic caliphate in the seventh to eighth centuries? Traditionally, historians have drawn on medieval sources and images to describe Islam as a "religion of the sword." More recently, it has been suggested that the bubonic plague—which struck in 541–542, during the reign of the Byzantine emperor Justinian, with sporadic outbreaks continuing through the first half of the eighth century—may have at least partly paved the way for the armies of the caliphate. The plague decimated traditional population centers in both Europe and Asia, which suggests that urban centers became relatively weaker while largely nomadic populations (as were many of the Arab tribes) became relatively stronger. This could be one explanation for the rapid progress made by the armies of the caliphate during this period in the Middle East, North Africa, Europe, and Central Asia.

The history of Central Eurasia in the sixth to eighth centuries is rather murky, probably owing to the effects of the same plague that afflicted other regions in this same period. In 552 the Kök Türks—a Turkic-speaking people from the area along the Orkhon River in Mongolia—established an empire stretching across the entire Eurasian steppe from Mongolia to the Black Sea region. Probably this was the first Turkic-speaking state that embraced all these territories (including Central Asia and the Black Sea region), and its establishment marked the beginning of a gradual process of "Turkification" of the peoples of these territories. That process would continue a millennium and a half down to our own times. The unity of the Kök Türk Empire (whose ruler was known as a *kaghan*) would be short-lived, however. By the late sixth century there were divisions in the empire, which soon fractured into what we know as the Western Türk confederation and the Eastern Türk confederation. The Western Türk confederation ceased to exist in the mid-seventh century, while the Eastern Türk confederation reemerged as a strong state from the 680s until its conquest by another Turkic people, the Uygurs, in 745.

The collapse of the Western Türk confederation was followed by the emergence of the powerful Turkic-speaking Khazar state, which would dominate the region of Western Eurasia until its conquest by Russia in 965. (Thereafter the Khazars are mentioned as a much weaker entity through the 11th century.) The Khazar state, whose capital was the city of Etil on the lower Volga River, was a commercial empire that welcomed merchants of diverse faiths, language groups, and countries (especially Byzantium).

Beginning in 642 the Khazars came into conflict with the armies of the Islamic caliphate, which had already seized control of the South Caucasus (also known as Transcaucasia, including the territory of present-day Azerbaijan). The fighting ended in 737, when the Khazar ruler was defeated and converted temporarily to Islam. Hostilities soon resumed, however, and by the late eighth century the ruler of the Khazars converted to Judaism.

The historical importance of the Khazar state was that it controlled the strategic pass at Derbent (on the coast of the Caspian Sea in present-day Dagestan). Many historians have speculated that by preventing the armies of the caliphate from moving north across the Caucasus Mountains, the Khazars kept Russia from becoming a Muslim state in this period. Even so, the earliest period of the Islamization of the North Caucasus is said to date from this time.

Although the armies of the caliphate were stopped in the Caucasus Mountains by the Khazars, there were no such barriers to expansion into Central Asia. We know quite a bit about the cultures of the ancient cities

A man examines some of the Islamic tombstones that are common in the ancient city of Derbent. This community on the Caspian Sea, where the Khazars held back the Arab Muslims in the seventh and eighth centuries, is more than 5,000 years old.

of Central Asia in this period. Bukhara, Samarkand, and other cities were home to peoples speaking Iranian languages such as Sogdian and practicing diverse religions such as **Zoroastrianism**, Buddhism, and Christianity. The reputation of the Sogdians was as merchants who traveled widely from the Black Sea peninsula of Crimea (a home to diverse peoples where religions such as Christianity and Judaism coexisted) in the west to China in the east.

Following earlier ineffectual raids in the late seventh century, the Arab general Qutayba ibn Muslim led the first serious campaigns from Merv into Central Asia from 705 until his death in 715. He was the first to establish Muslim rule in the land known as Transoxiana. The cities of Baykand, Bukhara, and Samarkand and the region of Khwarezm were captured in this early period. Ibn Muslim's death in the Fergana Valley delayed further expansion of the Islamic caliphate in Central Asia by roughly a century. The defeat of the Chinese armies at Talas (in present-day Kyrgyzstan) in 751 was an important turning point in ensuring a permanent Muslim presence in Central Asia. It was also an important moment in the development of Islamic civilization, because the capture of Chinese artisans led to the introduction of papermaking to the Islamic world. This transfer of technology would allow the reproduction of books at far lower cost than was possible previously.

During the period of the Samanid state in the 9th to 10th centuries, Arabic was introduced as a language of civilization in Central Asia, and Bukhara became the "dome" of Islamic civilization in the east. Bukhara was home to a number of important scholars whose legacy is important for the entire Muslim world today. The religious scholar Bukhari (810–869) compiled the *Sahih*, a canonical collection of the sayings (or Hadith) attributed to the prophet Muhammad, which is one of the core texts for Islamic religious law (Sharia). The impact of Arabic language and culture on the native Iranian dialects of the region was also a powerful factor in the emergence in Central Asia of New Persian as the second great Islamic literary language through the works of Rudaki (d. 941) and Firdawsi (d. 1020).

The Samanids, who had numerous Turkish military slaves in their service, were also active in trying to convert the Turkic nomads to their north. It was under Bukharan influence that Satuk Bughra Khan (d. 955) converted to Islam with 200,000 tents of Turks sometime in the first half of the 10th century. Satuk Bughra Khan was a member of a dynasty that modern scholars refer to as the Karakhanids. The Karakhanids established the first

Turkic Muslim state in the territory of present-day Kyrgyzstan and western Xinjiang (Kashgaria). Bukhara finally fell to the Karakhanids in 999.

Under the Karakhanids, Bukhara and other cities in Central Asia continued to make great contributions to Islamic civilization, first in works written in Arabic, and later increasingly in works written in Persian and even Turkic. Ibn Sina (980–1037), who was born near Bukhara and educated there, made major contributions to Islamic philosophy through his study of Greek philosophy and science, including the works of Aristotle. His classic textbook on medicine, translated into Latin in the 11th century

This blue-domed mosque is in Bukhara, a Central Asian city in present-day Uzbekistan. During the medieval period, Bukhara flourished as a center of Islamic learning and culture, with scholars like Ibn Sina and al-Biruni making great contributions to Islamic law, philosophy, and literature.

as the *Canon* of Avicenna (the name by which he was known in Latin), was used as a textbook in Europe for many centuries. Other scholars from Khwarezm include al-Biruni (973–1048), a polymath who made contributions in the fields of mathematics, astronomy, medicine, and history, and al-Khwarezmi (ca. 780–ca. 850), a natural scientist, mathematician, and astronomer whose name gives us the word *algorithm*. The rise of a Muslim Turkic literary culture and civilization in the late 11th century can also be seen through the famous Turkic-Arabic dictionary by Mahmud Kashgari and the mirror (or model) for princes known as the *Wisdom of Royal Glory,* written by Yusuf Khass Hajib.

Although the Khazars blocked the path for the expansion of the Islamic caliphate through the Caucasus, eventually Central Asia became the preferred route for contacts between the caliphate and Western Eurasia. The most important fruit of these contacts was the conversion of the Volga Bulgarian state to Islam by the early 10th century. The early history of the Volga Bulgars is unclear, but it is likely connected with the Khazar defeat of the previous Bulgar state in the south in the late seventh century. With the migration of some Bulgar groups to the north, the Volga Bulgarian state came into existence in the Middle Volga region, near the confluence of the Volga and Kama Rivers; it was a vassal state subject to the Khazars. (A second group of Bulgars migrated to the Balkans, lending their name to the present-day Slavic Bulgarians, while another migrated to the North Caucasus and is probably related to the present-day Balkars.)

We know a great deal about Volga Bulgaria because of the account of Ibn Fadlan, who traveled through Central Asia to the Middle Volga region as part of a diplomatic mission sent by the caliph in Baghdad in 921. Ibn Fadlan found a state with several towns, a mixed nomadic-agricultural economy, and a small Muslim population. Its ruler, Almush ibn Shilki, was already knowledgeable about the tenets of Islam. This state was a far northern outpost in the important medieval commerce in furs and other

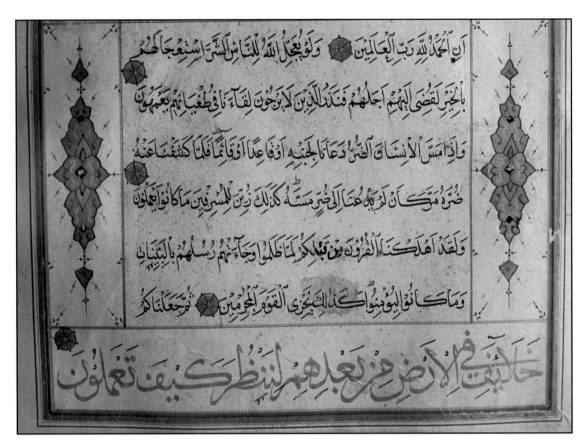

An ornate page from the Qur'an, which Muslims believe is the word of Allah (God) given directly to His prophet, Muhammad, through a series of revelations.

goods. The ruler was eager to strengthen his ties with the caliphate, in part to seek help in the construction of a fort against his overlords in the south—the Jewish Khazars, to whom he was paying tribute of one sable skin per household in his kingdom.

By the year 1200, Muslim communities were well established in the Crimea, the South Caucasus, parts of the North Caucasus, the Middle Volga region, and the sedentary regions of Central Asia. It is not clear to what extent the nomads of the Eurasian steppe might have been Muslim (though the Ghuzz, ancestors of the Turkmen, were already nominally Muslim in the early 10th century, according to Ibn Fadlan's account). It is also not clear that there were any Muslim communities yet in Siberia. In addition to the Muslim Turkic peoples, there were also smaller groups of Buddhist, Manichaean, Nestorian Christian, and Jewish Turkic peoples, as well as groups of Turkic peoples who were still following shamanism.

Islamization in the Early Medieval Period

Islamization meant different things in different places in medieval Eurasia. Written works of Arabic-language Islamic civilization were imported to Central Asia from the political centers of the caliphate—including Mecca, Damascus, and Baghdad—which meant that the political centers of Central Asia shared in the same high level of Islamic civilization. At the same time, the growing trend toward a new synthesis between Arabic Islamic civilization and the local languages and cultures led to the development of an equally high Persian-language Islamic civilization in Central Asia and Iran. From the 11th century on, it led to the development of a Turkic-language Islamic civilization in Central Asia (and later elsewhere in Eurasia).

Each culture that converted to Islam accepted the new religion on a foundation of its own culture, which usually included elements of earlier religious traditions. Iran was officially a Zoroastrian state before it became a Muslim state. Zoroastrianism was also practiced in Central Asia, as were Buddhism, Christianity, and later Manichaeism and Judaism. In the modern cultures of Iran and Central Asia there are many survivals of earlier folk traditions related, for example, to the celebration of the Iranian New Year (*Navruz*) on the vernal equinox, which marks the first day of spring. Other aspects of Central Asian Islam, such as the ritual use of fire, probably relate to earlier religious traditions associated with Zoroastrianism, in which fire has an important ritual value.

The nomadic populations of the Eurasian steppe region as well as the peoples of northern forest zones had their own traditional belief system or

Tourists visit a Zoroastrian fire temple near Baku, Azerbaijan. Islam spread throughout Asia in a syncretistic fashion, and elements of Muslim worship were often combined with rituals and features of earlier religions like Zoroastrianism.

religion based on worship of the spirits of natural phenomena (the sky, the earth, mountains, forests, groves of trees, thunder, and so on) and veneration of the spirits of ancestors. This is generally called shamanism, after the shaman (holy man) who is the intercessor with the spirits of the other world. Some scholars also think that the Turkic and Mongol peoples believed in the primacy of the sky god (or *tengri*). As various Turkic peoples converted to Islam, many of the underlying beliefs of their specific local cultures continued, lending a special character to the Islam practiced by individual Turkic peoples today. Probably in the early period, the role of the shamans or other members of society with a religious function continued largely unchanged. This helps to explain certain aspects of the later development of **Sufi orders**, including esoteric religious practices and veneration of religious shrines. The Sufi orders would also become very active as missionaries. For these reasons, it can be said that since the earliest conversion of local populations to Islam, the "high tradition" of Islam existed side by side with the popular or folk tradition, and in many cases became inseparable from it.

The Later Medieval Period

One of the most significant events in the history of both the Muslim and the non-Muslim communities of Central Eurasia was the establishment of the Mongol Empire. The founder of the empire was a poor youth in Mongolia named Temüjin who was able to attract followers and later client tribes in the latter half of the 12th century. Temüjin (ca. 1167–1227), who was declared supreme ruler with the Mongolian title *Chinggis Khan* (Genghis Khan) in 1206, organized the tribes under his leadership into a formidable military force. His armies conquered much of northern China, much of present-day Russia, and Central Asia as far west as the Aral Sea. Chinggis Khan's descendants greatly expanded the Mongol Empire, conquering all of China and pushing into the Middle East and central Europe.

Much has been written in the medieval chronicles about the brutality of the Mongols. Some of it must be true, but some of it—for example, the reports of millions of inhabitants killed in cities such as Herat or Nishapur, which likely did not have a million inhabitants—was no doubt an exaggeration. This problem is not limited to the Islamic sources: in the Russian chronicles, many of the brief early reports on the Mongol campaigns were embellished in later centuries. Based on these sensationalist medieval accounts, some modern historians have

Chinggis Khan (better known in the West as Genghis Khan) was perhaps the greatest conqueror the world has ever known. By the time of his death, the Mongols ruled most of Asia. His descendants would continue to expand the Mongol Empire during the 13th and 14th centuries.

also stressed the brutality of the Mongols. In addition, they have emphasized the "parasitic" character of the Mongol Empire based primarily on the fact that it collected taxes and raised armies (not unlike modern states!).

Much of Central Asia (Transoxiana, Kashgaria, Semirechie, Jungaria) was assigned by Chinggis Khan as a **patrimony** (*ulus*) to his second son, Chaghatay; it is known as the Chaghatay Khanate. The history of the Chaghatay Khanate reinforces many of the popular stereotypes concerning the Mongols. Although the cities of Central Asia were large and important centers of Islamic civilization, there is evidence to suggest that the Mongols thought of the territory primarily as pasturage for their horses. One 13th-century source, Juvayni's *History of the World Conqueror*, is full of accounts of Mongol atrocities against the populations of the cities during the early campaigns. Another source reports that, on his way to attack the Il-Khanate in Iran, Boraq Khan (1264–1270) did not hesitate to plunder the cities of Bukhara and Samarkand—in his own khanate. But some of these accounts must be taken with a grain of salt. While it is true that the Mongol rulers in the Chaghatay Khanate continued to follow a nomadic way of life and adhere to shamanism much longer than did the ruling elites in the other **Chinggisid** states, the major cities of Central Asia retained their status as leading centers of Islamic learning—which could not have been the case if all the accounts of Mongol depredations were true. The first Muslim Chinggisid ruler in the Chaghatay Khanate was Tarmashirin, and he was deposed by his decidedly anti-Islamic tribal leaders in 1334.

If the history of the Chaghatay Khanate reinforces many of the popular stereotypes concerning the Mongols, a new examination of the history of the Golden Horde serves as a counter-example to these very same stereotypes. The Golden Horde was assigned as a patrimony by Chinggis Khan to his eldest son, Jöchi. It consisted of territories of the Eurasian steppe and beyond, including Khwarezm in Central Asia. The first Mongol invasion of the territories of Russia took place in the period 1221–1224. In 1227, following Jōchi's death and shortly before his own death, Chinggis Khan assigned the eastern half of Jōchi's patrimony to Jōchi's eldest son, Orda; he assigned the western half to Jōchi's second son, Batu, who would consolidate his rule over the western patrimony beginning in the 1230s. (It should be noted that the Golden Horde was not known by this name until the 16th century or later. Orda's patrimony was known as the Blue Horde, and Batu's as the White Horde. There is much controversy over these names.)

Accounts by the European envoys John of Plano Carpini and William of Rubruck suggest that, as early as the 1240s or 1250s, the ruling elite of the Golden Horde was encouraging international commerce. The state provided security for merchants and taxed commerce; the cities of the still-nomadic rulers provided markets. By the late 13th century the Italian maritime republics of Venice, Genoa, and Pisa became involved in the Black Sea trade, some of which was negotiated directly with the Mongol rulers. The territories of the Golden Horde grew wheat and provided fish. Another important commodity was slaves, drawn mostly from the local population (especially the Christian Turkic Cumans). Some were children sold by their families; others, particularly in the North Caucasus, were subjects sold by their rulers. The net result of this extensive commerce supported by the rulers of the Golden Horde was a flow of money into their coffers from trade and taxation of commerce. This also led to the creation of permanent capital cities, first Saray (also known as Saray Batu) close to the mouth of the Volga River, and later New Saray (also known as Saray Berke) further upstream, which reduced the portage necessary to reach the Don River from the Volga River. Islamic civilization flourished in the sedentary centers in the Crimea and the Lower and Middle Volga regions (including the city of Bulgar) during this period thanks to the patronage of the Golden Horde rulers.

Sufi orders were active in the territories of the Golden Horde and played the role of Islamic missionaries. The first Golden Horde ruler to convert to Islam was Berke Khan (ruled 1255–1266). The role of Shaykh Sayf ad-Din Bakharzi in his conversion was reported in contemporary sources and glorified in later legends. Reports suggest that Töde Mengü Khan (ruled 1280–1287) was interested in mystical Islam. Finally, Islam became the state religion of the Golden Horde under Özbek Khan (also spelled Uzbek; ruled 1313–1341). There are contemporary reports and later legends concerning the role of a Sufi **shaykh** in his conversion, too. (Of course, as we know from European sources and the *Codex Cumanicus*, a locally produced work in Latin, Persian, and Cuman—a Kipchak Turkic dialect closest to modern Karachay—German and Italian missionaries were also active in the Golden Horde on behalf of the Catholic Church.)

From the accounts of the North African traveler Ibn Battuta, who visited the region in the 1330s, it is apparent that Sufi orders were active in the Crimea and the Caucasus as well as in Khwarezm. In the Crimea, Ibn Battuta visited a number of mosques, including one built in 1288 with the assistance of the Egyptian ruler Baybars and another built by Özbek Khan in 1314. Saray Berke was a large city with 13 mosques for Friday congregational prayers and many smaller mosques that attracted religious scholars of different legal schools from around the Muslim world. Ibn Battuta describes great centers of Islamic learning in Khwarezm as well.

The patronage of pious rulers was a strong factor in the development of a new Islamic Turkic literature, though more works were produced in the territories of the Golden Horde, by far, in Arabic and Persian. The first important work written in the new Islamic Turkic literary language was Rabghuzi's *Qisas ül-enbiya'* ("Stories of the Prophets"), composed around 1310 in Ribat-i Oghuz in Turkistan for the local ruler Nasirüddin Toqbugha. The first half of this collection of stories (based in large measure on apocryphal traditions) is devoted to the earlier prophets recognized

Turkish Sufis perform an energetic dance, believing that through ecstatic activity they can draw closer to Allah. Sufi orders played an important role in the spread of Islam throughout Central Asia and Russia.

by Muslims, beginning with Adam; the second half is devoted to the prophet Muhammad and his Companions. In later centuries this work would prove extremely popular in Russia.

The patronage of the khan's court also led to the development of a court literature in New Saray. The first major work in the new Islamic Turkic literary language of the Golden Horde to be connected with the court of the Golden Horde was Qutb's *Khusrev ü Shirin* ("Chosroe and Shirin"). Dedicated to Tinibek Khan (ruled 1341–1342) and his wife Melike Khatun, this work is an adaptation for the court of the classic romantic poem written by the great poet Nizami in Persian in the late 12th century. Such works were also produced elsewhere in the Golden Horde; one example is Khwarezmi's *Mahabbetname*, dedicated to Muhammad Khojabek in 1353.

A very different kind of work of religious literature is represented by the *Nehj ül-feradis* ("The Clear Path to Heaven"), which was intended as a handbook of the Islamic religion. It is likely that the work was written in New Saray no later than 1358 by Muhammad ibn Muhammad ibn Khusrev al-Khwarezmi.

Thus, it is clear that by the mid-14th century, the Golden Horde was home to a vibrant Islamic civilization with many centers of Islamic worship throughout its territories. These centers existed not only in areas that had an earlier Islamic tradition, such as Central Asia, but also in cities established during the Mongol period. The Golden Horde boasted a diverse range of native scholars as well as scholars who had moved there from around the Islamic world. In addition to a body of works written in Arabic and Persian, there were also indigenous works written in a new Islamic Turkic literary language of the Golden Horde. Even at the end of life, the Muslims of the Golden Horde were buried with tombstones containing inscriptions in Arabic script with formulas in Arabic and local Turkic languages. In other words, by the mid-14th century Islam had established very deep roots in all those areas of Central Eurasia that would later have a Muslim population under the Russian Empire.

The Black Death and its Aftermath

The Black Death was an epidemic (the term *pandemic* is actually more appropriate) of recurring waves of bubonic plague beginning in the mid-14th century that spread from Alexandria, Egypt, and Sicily to most of Europe. As we know from Western Europe, the massive depopulation associated with the Black Death (up to 90 percent in some areas) resulted in a host of social, political, cultural, and economic consequences. Nevertheless, the Black Death has been largely neglected in the study of Central Eurasia (including Russia, the Golden Horde, and the Chaghatay Khanate), even though the Black Death spread to Egypt and Italy from

Kaffa in the Crimea. Sources document that before the Black Death arrived in Kaffa in 1346, it had earlier afflicted parts of Central Asia and the entire Volga region.

Recent scholarly examinations of the impact of the Black Death in the Chaghatay Khanate and the Golden Horde point to large-scale depopulation, instability of political structures, and cultural and technological regression. In the 1350s the Chaghatay Khanate split into an eastern territory (known as Mogholistan) and a western territory (Transoxiana). After about 1360 the Golden Horde disintegrated and fell into a period of civil war lasting decades. The new cities of the Golden Horde in the steppe zone rapidly declined and soon disappeared. The older cities of the region also declined, and it is possible that mid-14th-century descriptions of empty cities in Central Asia may be reporting the results of the plague. Accompanying the disappearance of states and cities during this period was the disappearance of a number of Turkic and non-Turkic literary languages, including the language written in Syriac script of Christian Turks around Lake Issyk-Kul (present-day Kyrgyzstan) and the language written in Arabic script of Muslim Volga Bulgarians in the Middle Volga region. No new works were produced in the Islamic Turkic literary language of the Golden Horde after this time, either. As the cities declined, the nomads of the steppe zone inevitably became relatively more powerful, since infectious disease typically spreads less effectively among a nomadic population. Finally, as we know from medieval Europe, the Black Death led to an increase in religiosity. In this respect we can understand "The Clear Path to Heaven," a work written during the time of the plague, as responding to the punishment from God that has been unleashed upon the Muslim population of the region. It is a work intended as a way to spread knowledge about Islam, as an act of religious devotion, and as an attempt to answer the question of how one might find a clear path to Heaven in such difficult times.

Dawn breaks over the tiled domes of Shah-i Zinda, a mausoleum in Samarkand where descendants of the famous Tatar conqueror Tamerlane (Timur the Lame) are buried. Tamerlane and his successors made the Central Asian city of Samarkand an important center of Islamic culture and civilization.

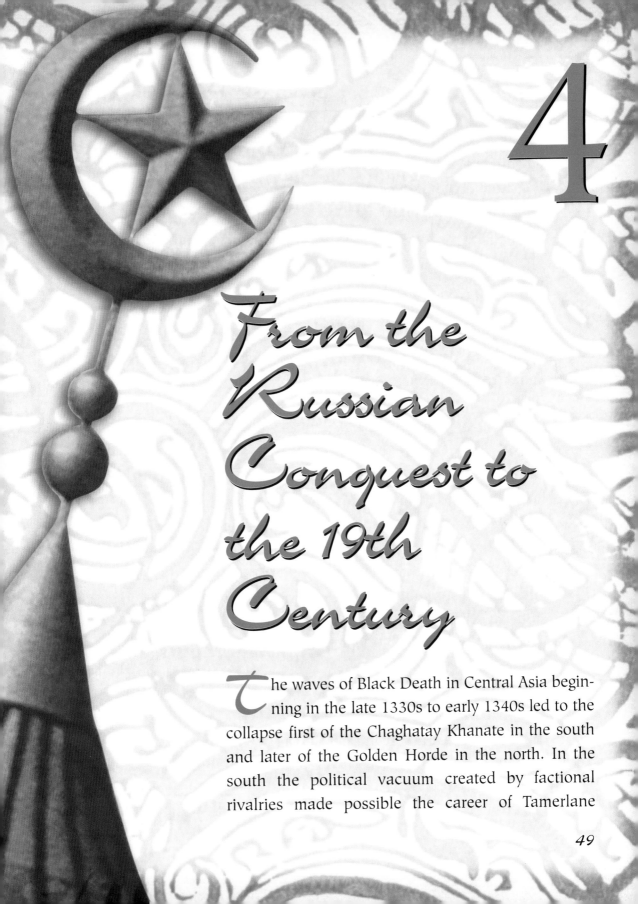

From the Russian Conquest to the 19th Century

4

he waves of Black Death in Central Asia beginning in the late 1330s to early 1340s led to the
collapse first of the Chaghatay Khanate in the south
and later of the Golden Horde in the north. In the
south the political vacuum created by factional
rivalries made possible the career of Tamerlane

(Timur-i Leng, or "Timur the Lame"). He began his career as leader of the Barlas tribe (rather than as a direct descendant of Chinggis Khan), but by the time of his death he had earned a reputation as a great conqueror. Beginning in 1380–1382, he expanded his campaigns beyond the territories of the former Chaghatay Khanate into Iran and Anatolia, followed by campaigns against the territories of the Golden Horde in the late 1380s and early 1390s. He also continued campaigns against Iran, Anatolia, the Caucasus, the Middle East, and India until his death in 1405.

Tamerlane transformed Samarkand into a greater city than ever before by making it his capital and redirecting transregional commerce from the northern Silk Road passing through the territories of the former Golden Horde to the southern Silk Road connecting the eastern Mediterranean through Iran to Samarkand. Tamerlane built up the markets of Samarkand and profited greatly from trade. His wealth allowed him to be the patron of great works of architecture in Samarkand in the complex of mausoleums that are still admired today. The achievements in Islamic art and literature of the period of Tamerlane and his successors (including works by Tamerlane's descendants) are still considered to represent one of the pinnacles of Islamic civilization. His grandson Ulughbek's famous **madrasa** in Samarkand was one of the most important centers of its time for science, especially in the fields of mathematics and astronomy, for the study of which it had its own observatory. The famous administrator, patron, and poet Ali Shir Navai (d. 1501) at the court of Sultan Husayn Bayqara in Herat is credited with reviving the Central Asian Islamic Turkic language that we call Chaghatay (also known as "Old Uzbek").

The heightened importance of nomadic confederations that survived the Golden Horde can be seen from the prominent nomadic confederations in the 15th and 16th centuries such as the Uzbek tribal confederation (named after Özbek Khan) and later the Nogay Horde. The Uzbek tribal confederation, also known as the Shaybanids (Shibanids), became increasingly involved in Central Asian affairs under the Chinggisid khans Abulkhayr (d. 1468) and Muhammad (d. 1510). They slowly drove the descendants of Tamerlane such as Shahrukh, Ulughbek, Husayn Bayqara, and Babur out of Samarkand in Transoxiana to Herat and eventually out of Central Asia altogether into India.

Following the Black Death, Islam became a second source of legitimacy for an aspiring Chinggisid khan or any other potential ruler. One of the notable features of Central Asian Islam under both the Timurids and Shaybanids was the prominent role of Central Asian Sufi orders such as the Kubraviya, the Naqshbandiya, and the Yasaviya. As at the court of Özbek Khan during the Golden Horde, Timurid and later Shaybanid rulers sought the company of Sufi thinkers such as the poet Jami

A statue of Tamerlane (1336–1405) in the city of Tashkent, in modern-day Uzbekistan.

(d. 1492) and Khoja Ubaydullah Ahrar (d. 1490). Over the 15th and 16th centuries, these orders became increasingly wealthy as they were lavished with gifts and entitlements by rulers seeking legitimacy through the support of the leaders of these religious orders. The influence of these Sufi orders would continue to expand beyond the borders of Central Asia in the following centuries.

In the north, while the two halves of the Golden Horde (the White Horde in the west and the Blue Horde in the east) ruled over a vast territory, after the collapse of the 1360s the continuing political unity of this vast territory was no longer possible. Beginning in the early 15th century we see the emergence of new regional states that could control only much smaller territories, no doubt a reflection of the significant decline in population that these territories had undergone. These new regional states or khanates came into existence in Kazan (1438), the Crimea (1449), Kasimov (1452), Astrakhan, and Tümen (Siberia). The Khanate of Kasimov would continue a quiet existence in the service of Russia. On the other hand, the Crimean Khanate, which became a protectorate of the Ottoman Empire in 1475 and maintained its own independent Giray line of Chinggisid khans, would continue its active participation in Central Eurasian affairs until the late 18th century.

As with the earlier Chinggisid states, each state was led by a Chinggisid khan, and had a special ruling council consisting of the leaders of the four most important regional tribes in addition to other tribal and sedentary populations. Following the Black Death factional rivalries among competing Chinggisids made Islam an equally important source of legitimacy for rulers. Therefore in each khanate Islamic religious officials, *seyyids* (descendants of the prophet Muhammad), and other religious figures connected with the tribes had a special role. Although each of these khanates was independent, there were close relationships between them through the ruling Chinggisid dynasty, with individuals often moving as khan from one state to another. There were also close relations between the ruling tribes of each state as well as close marital ties between the nomadic Nogay Horde, the khans, and the tribes. Limited surviving examples of poetic works influenced by **Sufism** and historical works from the regional khanates in this period show that an Islamic Turkic culture was once again thriving in these states. This was also a period in which the political system of Western Eurasia was fairly balanced among these regional khanates and Russia and there were thriving economic relations between these states.

The Conquest of the Khanate of Kazan and the Establishment of the Russian Empire

Historians of Russia disagree over which date marks the overthrow of the "Tatar Yoke," the disparaging term used in Russian for the period of Mongol domination over Russia. Was it at the Battle of Kulikovo Pole in 1380, or perhaps following the confrontation on the Ugra River in 1480? Actually Russia had a largely peaceful symbiotic relationship with the Golden Horde, even though it remained subject politically to the Chinggisid rulers. There was a thriving commerce over the Volga River, and the Russian Orthodox Church had its own representative in Saray. Later claims by national historians aside, this was arguably a prosperous period in Russian history, just as it was a prosperous period for the Golden Horde. The collapse of the Golden Horde was a direct result of the Black Death, not a result of conflict with Russia or any other state.

Russia's relationship with the successor khanates to the Golden Horde was qualitatively different because Russia's military might matched fairly evenly with the military might of the khanates; nor were relations always hostile. In fact, there were very active commercial relations between these states, and Russia's continuing expansion to the east and later to the south can be tied to an attempt to control trade. Whereas the Black Death weakened the descendants of Chinggis Khan by creating rivalries because of uncertainty over legitimate claims to succession, the same historical phenomenon actually strengthened Moscow by allowing the grand duke of Moscow to "gather the Russian lands" and thereby strengthen his power.

In the late 15th century Russian clerics began to formulate an ideology legitimating the conquest of the Khanate of Kazan as reflected in the compilations of new chronicle traditions laying claim to the territory of the khanate. Finally, in 1552, Ivan IV—also known as Ivan the Terrible—conquered the Khanate of Kazan. After that, in 1556, Russia conquered the

Khanate of Astrakhan in the south and the Siberian Khanate in the 1570s. Even though Russia never overthrew the "Tatar Yoke," it was through the conquest of the Khanate of Kazan that the ruler of Moscow became the "White Tsar," inheritor of the mantle of the ruler of the White Horde (the western patrimony of Batu in what we call today the Golden Horde). Russia was now a multi-ethnic, multi-religious empire.

Following the conquest of Kazan, in 1555–1576 the Russian administration began the first historical campaign of forced conversion of local Muslim Tatars to Christianity; those who refused had to live outside the city walls. The law code of 1649 prescribed the penalty of death for Muslims proselytizing Christians. The second campaign to convert Muslim Tatars to Christianity began under Tsar Peter the Great in the early 18th century, including missionary activity in their native Tatar language. A much harsher campaign to attack Islam began in 1740 with the creation of the Office for the Affairs of New Converts. In addition, there was a campaign to destroy newly built mosques and prohibit the further construction of new mosques. During this campaign, 418 of the 536 mosques in the Middle Volga region were destroyed. Although certain restrictions were occasionally eased, there was also a campaign to build

Under its tsar Peter the Great (1672–1725), Russia underwent a period of modernization and was transformed into a major European power.

churches in areas inhabited by Tatars and to force out the Tatars living in those neighborhoods. With the Muslim Tatars nearing revolt, the Office for the Affairs of New Converts was closed in 1764.

Persecution of the Muslims of the Russian Empire eased under Catherine II, known as Catherine the Great. While she still supported missionary activity among the Muslim Tatars, she was far less hostile to them than her predecessors. She enacted laws in 1763 and 1776 allowing Muslim Tatars to engage in commerce, as a result of which a Tatar commercial class and a *diaspora* engaged in commerce in Central Asia began to develop. This led to greater contacts between the Middle Volga region and Central Asia, with many families sending their sons for a madrasa education in Bukhara or one of the other

Unlike her predecessors, Catherine the Great (1729–1796) permitted Muslims in the Russian Empire to practice their religion with fewer restrictions.

seats of Islamic learning in Central Asia. In 1773 there was an edict by the Holy Synod proclaiming "Toleration of All Faiths," which allowed Muslims to build new mosques and madrasas. Catherine also established in Ufa a *muftiate* (a *mufti* is an Islamic scholar who makes legal rulings) governing the Muslims of the Russian Empire, which was the first time a chief religious official of the Muslims of the Russian Empire was recognized by the state. (In 1872 Russia would also establish a muftiate in Baku to complement the two existing muftiates in Orenburg and Bakhchesaray in the

Crimea.) In 1786 Catherine also authorized the expansion of Islamic institutions (staffed by Muslim Tatars) in the Bashkir and Kazakh steppes. This paved the way for a boom in Muslim publishing in the 19th century, beginning with the establishment of the first Muslim Tatar publishing house in Kazan in 1800.

Expansion South into the Crimea, the Caucasus, and Central Asia

Russia's involvement in the North Caucasus dates to Ivan the Terrible's alliance with the rulers of Kabarda in 1557. For a half century Russia sought closer relations with the various peoples of the North Caucasus, establishing a fortress in Dagestan in 1594, but it was wiped out in 1605. Beginning in the late 16th century, Cossacks (irregular Orthodox Christian Slavic troops) settled along the Terek River (northeast Caucasus), and in the 17th century along the Kuban' River (northwest Caucasus). While the Cossacks served to represent the interests of Russia and Orthodox Christianity, in fact they also had close social, cultural, and economic ties with the local peoples, who exerted a lasting influence on Cossack culture, including their clothing.

The Persian campaign of Peter the Great in 1722 was another attempt to exert Russian influence on the Caucasus. While the Russian fleet was able to capture Derbent (present-day Dagestan) and Baku (present-day Azerbaijan) in 1732–1735, Russia was forced to recognize Iranian domination over the Caspian Sea region in the Treaty of Ganja in 1735 and withdrew from these cities. Russia established a series of outposts in the North Caucasus in the mid-18th century. With the Treaty of Küchük Kaynarja in 1774, Russia gained the Crimean Khanate and Kabarda from the Ottoman Empire. Russia conquered the Crimea beginning in 1783 and annexed Kabarda in 1806. Russia's authority over Dagestan and in the South Caucasus territories in present-day Azerbaijan, eastern Armenia, and Georgia was recognized by Iran in the Treaty of Gulistan (1813), after which Russia built a series of military outposts throughout the North Caucasus.

Russia's conquest of the mountain peoples of the North Caucasus began in the 1770s. In contrast to the ease with which it had brought the Kabarda and part of Dagestan under its control, Russia now entered into a long and bloody guerrilla war with the Muslim Chechen, Avar, Adyge, Abaza, Abadzekh, Ubykh, Bzhadug, Nabukhay, and Shapsug peoples. It faced the anti-Russian resistance movement of the Chechen Sufi shaykh Mansur Ushurma (1785–1791). In 1825 the politico-religious leaders of the North Caucasian anti-colonial movement proclaimed a holy war (*ghazavat*) against the Orthodox Christian invaders, which spread throughout Chechnya and Dagestan. In this period the religious leaders advocated the religious and political independence of North Caucasian Muslims in an independent state (*imamate*) based on Islamic religious law (Sharia) and a rejection of the strict local pre-Islamic customs (*adat*). The most famous of the leaders of this anti-colonial resistance during the period 1834–1859 was Imam Shamil (d. 1871), who remained a symbolic figure for the resistance even after his capture. The Russian capture of Shamil was aided by a lack of unity among the North Caucasians, some of whom were ready to cooperate with the Russians. There were no further successful uprisings after 1859, though anti-colonial sentiment remains in the region until this very day. Just as was the case after the fall of the Crimean Khanate, large numbers of North Caucasians fled to the Ottoman Empire after the Russian conquest on the principle that their original homeland was now *Dar al-harb*, a territory ruled by the infidels (as opposed to *Dar al-islam*).

The close link between religion and anti-colonial resistance in the North Caucasus is related to the strong influence of the Naqshbandi Sufi order in the North Caucasus. Strong personal ties between *shaykh* ("teacher") and *murid* ("disciple") and the secretive organization of Sufi orders were normally for the communication of esoteric religious knowledge. But they also served the purposes of anti-colonial resistance and guerrilla war equally well. Shamil was himself both a political leader as well as the disciple of Jamal al-Din, a Naqshbandi shaykh from Dagestan. Even in the 1990s, the victory celebrations of Chechen warriors resembled a *dhikr* (in local languages of Russia *zikr*, the ritual repetitive chanting of a religious formula as a part of the process of achieving religious ecstasy).

Russia's first expedition into Central Asia to establish relations with the Khanate of Khiva (in Khwarezm) ended in disaster in 1717. Russian expansion into the Kazakh steppe then began in 1730 with the declaration of fealty to Russia by Abilay Khan of the Lesser Horde, one of the three major Kazakh hordes (*zhüz*) of the time. In the second half of the 18th century Russia began creating military outposts and settlements along the fringe of the Kazakh steppe. In the 1770s Russia also adopted a policy of sending Tatar *mullahs* ("clerics") to teach the Kazakhs more about Islam in an effort to secure better control over them, and Zhangir Khan of the Bükey Horde issued a decree in 1823 promoting the establishment of mosques and schools (*mekteb*). The Kazakh hordes were finally subjugated between 1822 and 1848 (the Middle Horde in 1822, the Lesser Horde in 1824, the Bükey Horde in 1845, and the Greater Horde in 1848), and Russia established the colonial capital of Vernyi (the future Almaty) in 1853.

The Russian colonial presence in the Kazakh steppe had profound consequences for the Kazakhs (whom the Russians mistakenly called "Kyrgyz" in this period). The growing Slavic and German colonization of the steppe meant first of all that the largely nomadic Kazakhs were suddenly losing access to more and more of their best grazing lands. The monetary taxes imposed on the formerly self-sufficient nomads forced them to seek means to earn money. The Russians also imposed an unfamiliar system of electing local leaders and permanent judges to serve under the Russian administrators, a system that bred corruption. In the mid-19th century some Kazakhs began to attend Russian schools. One brilliant example of this was Chokan Valikhanov (ca. 1837–1865), who befriended famous Russian scholars and writers while serving the Russian colonial administration and left a body of important scholarly works on his own people.

A Russian man stands in a cotton field somewhere in the Caucasus, circa 1905. As the Russian Empire expanded into Central Asia, settlers in the territories were encouraged to raise cotton and other crops that would enrich the empire.

The Russian conquest of the rest of Central Asia (the Khanate of Khiva, the Emirate of Bukhara, the Khanate of Kokand, and the Turkmen), from the taking of Tashkent (present-day Uzbekistan) in 1864 to the capture of Merv (present-day Turkmenistan) in 1884, has a complex series of underlying factors. By the mid-19th century the European powers were in competition with one another in other parts of the world, and in Central Asia the Russians hoped to stop any further British expansion to the north. But Russia was also anxious for Central Asian cotton to supply its textile mills in the north, and following the conquest Russian factories also flooded Central Asia with manufactured goods, wiping out local textile and craft production. In order to justify their colonial expansion they also explained that these "Oriental" civilizations were in decline and not able to govern themselves. One of the rationalizations that European powers, including Russia, offered for their expansion into other parts of the world was their "civilizing mission," which usually meant spreading Christianity among Muslims and other "heathens." They also developed the ideology of "Muslim fanaticism" that needed to be countered. In fact, while Governor-General von Kaufman eliminated the chief religious official (*shaykh ul-Islam*) and the chief Islamic judge (*kazi-kalan*) and banned the activities of the religious police, including enforcement of Sharia, he otherwise followed a policy of ignoring Muslims. He allowed them to practice their own religion, but Islamic institutions were not going to be protected by the secular colonial administration. For the Russians, the Emirate of Bukhara was another matter altogether. It was deemed so "fanatic" that its status remained that of a vassal state of Russia ruled by its own emir.

In the early 19th century there was a renewed effort to convert Muslim Tatars to Orthodox Christianity through publications in their own language. New economic incentives to convert to Christianity were offered in

1849 in the form of exemption from various forms of taxation, some for life. Despite these efforts, and the prohibitions against **apostasy,** many of the communities of new converts to Christianity in the 18th century had returned to Islam by the early 19th century. As in earlier periods, one of the responses of the state was to order the resettlement of Muslim Tatars among Christians.

There is ample evidence to suggest that the "apostasy" of the Christianized Tatars reverting to their earlier religion was part of the broader phenomenon of the "re-Islamization" of the Middle Volga region in the 18th and 19th centuries. This re-Islamization is connected with the missionary activities of *ishans* ("religious teachers" or "shaykhs") belonging to the Naqshbandi order originating in Central Asia. Perhaps this heightened missionary activity grew from Catherine the Great's policies in the 1760s leading to increased contacts between the Muslim Tatars of the Middle Volga region and seats of Islamic learning in Central Asia such as Bukhara and Samarkand, which were at the same time major nodes of the Naqshbandi order.

Although there was certainly a "missionary Islam" of Sufi orders present on the territories of the Golden Horde in the early 14th century (based upon the account of Ibn Battuta), what we know of Islam in the Golden Horde in the 14th century (as in "The Clear Path to Heaven") suggests a first-hand familiarity with an orthodox brand of Islam based on its classical sources. Poetry from the Khanate of Kazan reflects a familiarity with mystical Islamic poetry, but that was universal for the high style of Islam Turkic poetry of the time. What we find in the re-Islamization of Christianized Tatars in the mid-19th century is a heavy reliance on works of Tatar devotional literature—such as *Qissa-i Yusuf* ("The Story of Joseph"), *Kesikbash kitabi* ("The Decapitated Head"), *Akhir zaman kitabi* ("The Book of the End of Time"), and *Bädävam kitabi* ("The Book of Forever")—popular among Sufis. Also instrumental were catechisms (short collections of prayers) such as *Shärait ül-iman* (also known popularly as *Iman sharti*), as well as spiritual songs (*mönäjät*), which could be learned even by the illiterate. (It has also been noted that the educational program of the bearers of Sufi Islam in the Middle Volga region foreshadows the later movement for educational reform among the Muslims of the Russian Empire.)

Such a concept of the re-Islamization of the Middle Volga region by the Naqshbandi Sufi order is consistent with the wide popularity enjoyed in this period by Rabghuzi's "Stories of the Prophets" (14th century), which was printed in more copies than any other work published in Tatar in the Middle Volga region during this period. Among Tatars, Rabghuzi's work was an essential text in the popular vernacular devotional literature (as opposed to works in Arabic such as the Qur'an), which formed the core of the Sufi approach to Islam in the Middle Volga region. (On a personal note, my own mother, whose Mishär Tatar parents were originally from a village in the Penza *gubernia*, would regularly read from Rabghuzi's "Stories of the Prophets" as a part of her religious devotion, and it would not be an exaggeration to say that this work formed the core of her understanding of Islam.)

A new chapter in the Russian Empire's policies against Muslim Tatars is linked with the career of Nikolai I. Il'minskii, who advocated using education in all local languages to help convert Muslims to Orthodox Christianity as well as to Russify them. Il'minskii was opposed to using only Tatar in schools, since he did not want all Muslims to learn Tatar as a language that might serve to politically unite them. He recommended that Muslim schools be required to hire Russian teachers at their own expense, but the idea of learning Russian was **anathema** to many Muslims at the time. His program was officially approved in 1870. In Central Asia his program of opening native language schools was pursued by his disciple, Ibray Altinsarin.

To this point in history, the Muslims of the Russian Empire were incorporated into the empire as voluntary or forced subjects. They struggled to practice their own faith, despite attempts by the state to forcibly convert them in various periods. Their resistance was through their faith as Muslims and, especially later, through the leadership of networks of Sufis who were teachers or even political and military leaders of anti-colonial resistance. The next chapter will describe what happened when the Muslims began to internalize and respond to the culture of their rulers.

A family of Kyrgyz (Kazakh) nomads sits on the steppes of the Russian Empire, circa 1895.

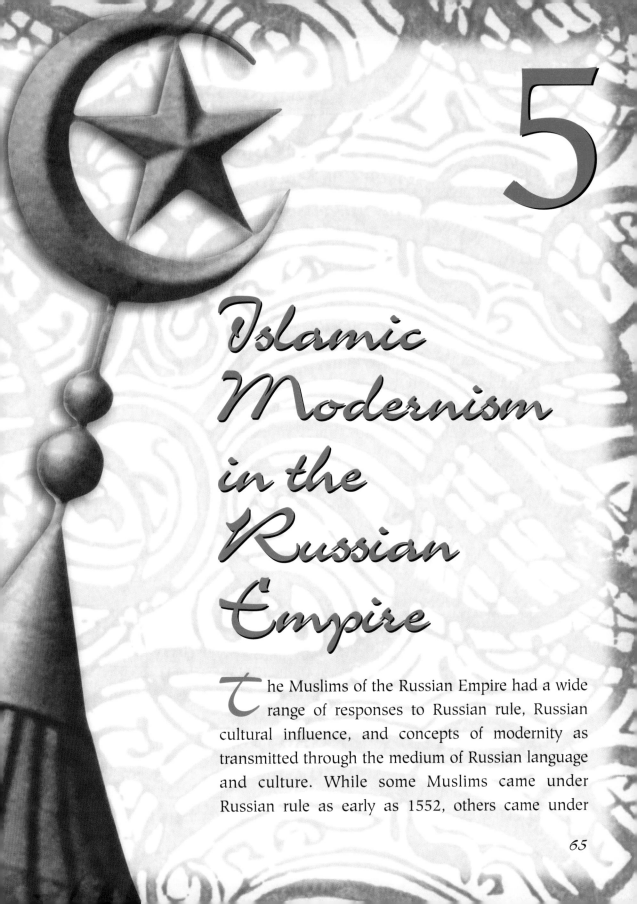

5

Islamic Modernism in the Russian Empire

The Muslims of the Russian Empire had a wide range of responses to Russian rule, Russian cultural influence, and concepts of modernity as transmitted through the medium of Russian language and culture. While some Muslims came under Russian rule as early as 1552, others came under direct Russian (or, more accurately, Soviet) rule only after 1917. In some areas Muslims began to express new ideas concerning educational, religious, social, and political reform in the late 18th century, subsequently entering into dialogue with international Islamic movements of the era. In other areas Muslims did not embrace such new ideas until the early 20th century. The total picture of this history of Islamic reform is poorly understood in many fundamental respects.

Perhaps the earliest critique of traditional education in Bukhara was by the Tatar religious scholar and poet Abdärrähim Utiz Imäni al-Bulghari (1754–1834). In one of his works, probably composed while he was still a student in Bukhara (he returned to the Middle Volga region in 1795), he describes the corruption of religious teachers in Bukhara's madrasas. In another work al-Bulghari stressed the importance of education.

Another important Tatar intellectual who studied in Bukhara and railed against ignorant religious scholars was Abdännasir Qursavi (1776–1812). It was commonly believed that independent interpretation of the Qur'an and Islamic religious law (*ijtihad*) was no longer possible after the end of the "classical period" of Islam. In his *Irshad li-l-ibad* ("Guide to the Faithful"), written in Arabic, Qursavi argued for the need to reject this doctrine of the "closure of independent interpretation." (This is an important early precedent for a discussion that is taking place in the Muslim world today, after the events of September 11, 2001.) In 1808 Qursavi returned to Bukhara to debate his views with local scholars, for which he was sentenced to death for apostasy. He narrowly escaped with his life, and accusations that he was an infidel followed him back to Kazan.

Qursavi's ideas had a profound impact on Shihabäddin Märjani (1818–1889), another Tatar religious scholar who studied in Bukhara and Samarkand and was critical of what he saw there. Märjani, one of the leading Muslim intellectuals in the Russian Empire in the 19th century, put forth the following reform program, for which he is well known:

1. Freedom of *ijtihad* or interpretation of religious law, with individuals making their own responses to every question based on their own understanding of the Qur'an.

2. Abandonment of blind submission to the traditional authorities (*taqlid*).

Various interpretations of Islamic teachings are noted in the margins of this book containing legal opinions, which dates from the year 808. By the 11th century, it was commonly accepted that independent interpretation of the Qur'an and the Hadith—primary sources for Islamic law—was no longer possible. Muslim scholars refer to this as the closure of the gate of *ijtihad* (independent reasoning). During the late 18th century and early 19th century, Tatar religious scholars like Abdännasir Qursavi argued that Muslims should be permitted to reinterpret Islamic law.

3. Rejection by the madrasas of books of scholastic conservative philosophy.

4. Teaching of the Qur'an, the Hadith, and the history of Islam in the madrasas.

5. Teaching of science and Russian language in the madrasas.

6. Return to Islamic culture and the purity of early Islam.

Perhaps the most significant aspect of Islam in Russia during the first half of the 19th century is that it produced ideas about educational and religious reform that were unknown elsewhere in the Muslim world at the time. In other words, the earliest ideas for modernizing Islam came from the Muslims of the Russian Empire.

The Rise of Publishing in the Local Dialects

Around 1800 the major Arabic-script literary languages in use among the Muslim Turks were Chaghatay (also known as "Old Uzbek") in Central Asia and the Middle Volga region, and classical Turkish (Ottoman Turkish and Azeri) in the Ottoman Empire and Azerbaijan. Both literary languages drew heavily on Arabic and Persian vocabulary. Arabic and Persian were also important scholarly languages that were in wide use at the time. By the middle of the 19th century, however, there was a growing interest in writing works in the local dialects.

The earliest modernizing writer in Azeri language and literature was Mirza Fäth Äli Ahundzade (1811–1878), who wrote comic plays in a European style. The works in the local Azeri dialect could be understood by all social classes (though he also wrote in other languages such as Persian). Another significant figure was Hasan Melikov-Zarbadi (1837–1907), who began to publish the Azeri-language newspaper *Ekinji* ("The Sower") in 1875. Although it was closed down by Russian authorities just two years later, *Ekinji* served as a model for future Azeri newspapers.

In the Middle Volga region Qayyum Nasiri (1824–1902) began his activities as a writer in 1854 with the goal of creating a new "Tatar" literary language. He began to collect and publish Tatar folk literature, and he also wrote grammars and a dictionary of Tatar. Later he wrote various books on geometry, geography, history, and natural science in this new literary language. Since he was not allowed to publish a newspaper, he began to publish an almanac called the "Kazan Calendar" in 1870. In this publication, which came out every three years until 1897, Nasiri included Tatar texts relating to folklore and to literary, historical, and social subjects. He strove to enlighten and introduce modern learning to his people, advocated the study of Russian, and laid the foundations of modern Kazan Tatar literature—all the while living in poverty. By the first decade of the 20th century, Tatar writers in the Middle Volga region such as Ayaz Iskhaki would be writing works of social criticism and confronting socialist ideas, while Muslims in other regions (especially Central Asia) were only beginning to confront ideas of modernity.

In the Kazakh steppe Ibray Altinsarin (1841–1899) wrote poems and introduced prose works that were retellings of Kazakh folktales or written under the influence of Russian literature. The greatest Kazakh intellectual of the era was Abay Qunanbay (1845–1904), who learned Arabic, Persian, and Chaghatay through a traditional Islamic education, but then became acquainted with Russian and European thinkers through study of the Russian language. In addition to the great original works that he wrote, he translated works from Russian into Kazakh.

In sedentary Central Asia there was a strong literary tradition in Chaghatay Turkic (which was closely tied to the local vernacular), in addition to a strong literary tradition in Persian. Therefore it is difficult to speak of a vernacular tradition that emerges in the mid-19th century. We can, however, point to the official organ of the Russian colonial administration, the *Turkistan Vilayatining Gazeti* ("Gazette of Turkistan

Province"), which began publishing in Chaghatay as well as in Kazakh in 1870.

The Emergence of Muslim Modernist Movements

The second half of the 19th century was a period of great ideas and movements among the Muslims of the Russian Empire, in particular the Muslim Turks. One of the greatest figures in the history of the Muslims of the Russian Empire flourished during this time: Ismail Gaspirali, also known as Ismail Gasprinsky (1851–1914). A Muslim Tatar born in the Crimea, Gaspirali made important contributions as an educator, publisher, and political thinker.

Shihabäddin Märjani's ideas in the field of education found resonance with Gaspirali, who had the important added benefit of studying in St. Petersburg, Paris, and Istanbul. Beginning in the late 1870s, Gaspirali introduced into his school in Bakhchesaray (in the Crimea) modern subjects such as history, geography, and mathematics, which were taught in Russian and Tatar, alongside the traditional Islamic subjects, which were taught in Arabic. He also developed a 30-day program for teaching literacy in the Arabic script, known as the "phonetic method." He even demonstrated this method in visits to other Muslim lands. Gaspirali's followers spread "New Method" schools throughout the Crimea, the Middle Volga region, and elsewhere in the Russian Empire, though they met with suspicion and resistance in Turkistan. While levels of literacy soared to about 11 percent in the Middle Volga region, in Turkistan they were under 1 percent at the turn of the century. The "New Method"—in Turkic, *Usul-i jädid*—gave rise to the term *Jadidism*, which is commonly used today to describe the reform movement of the era.

In addition to his advocacy of literacy and modern education, Gaspirali was important as a political thinker and publisher. In *Russkoye musul'manstvo,* or "The Muslims of Russia" (1881) and later works, he argued that Muslims naturally get along with Russians and could be good citizens of the Russian Empire. In 1883 he also began publishing in Bakhchesaray a landmark newspaper called *Terjüman/Perevodchik,* or "The Translator." It is primarily through this newspaper, which had readers all over the Ottoman Empire, the Russian Empire, and beyond that he later advocated his principle of "unity in language, thought, and action." His deep belief in the unity of the Muslim Turkic peoples was reflected in the language of the newspaper, which was, in fact, a project for creating a unified Islamic Turkic literary language for the Muslims of the Russian Empire (not unlike the linguistic unification of Germany or Italy in the 19th century). While he was advocating the unity of Muslim Turks within the Russian Empire and the unity of all Muslim Turks across empires, beyond the Turkic world he was advocating the unity of all Muslims. The authorities in the Russian Empire found such political ideas, labeled respectively "Pan-Turkism" and "Pan-Islamism," deeply unsettling. In particular, the concept of the unity of all Muslims tied into similar ideas expressed by anti-colonial Muslim intellectuals such as Jamal al-Din al-Afghani in the Middle East and South Asia. No wonder, then, that such ideas came to have very negative connotations in the Russian Empire of the late 19th and early 20th centuries. Surprisingly, these ideas continue to elicit negative responses in the post-Soviet space (comparable to the emotions surrounding the term *Fascism*).

Whereas Gaspirali advocated a non-territorially-based common identity for all the Muslim Turks and even all the Muslims of the Russian Empire, by the time of his death he was witness to the failure of his idea. Perhaps the main reason for this was the competing idea for a modern "Tatar" nation developed by Märjani beginning in the 1850s. In the 1870s and 1880s Märjani published works on Tatar history that developed a "national" history for the Muslim Turks of the Middle Volga region based on a national identity in the modern sense of a "territorial nation" whose members are linked by a common name, belief in a shared history, and the psychological sense of being a single community linked by their name and ancestry. Märjani argued that the Muslim Turks of the Middle Volga region should be proud to call themselves Tatar (a name that had come to be used by Russians to refer to all the non-Slavic, non-Christian populations of the Russian Empire from the Caucasus to Siberia). Further, he said, their history as Tatars extended in an unbroken line through the Muslims of Volga Bulgaria, the Golden Horde, and the Khanate of Kazan. Märjani's writings laid the foundation for the modern identity of the Kazan Tatars. His ideas would continue to find resonance among various intellectuals down to the time of the Bolshevik Revolution.

There was also a series of histories written in the late 18th century and the early 19th century referring to the peoples of the Middle Volga region as Bulgars. These problematic works stressed the Islamic ties of the peoples of the Middle Volga region and did not reflect a communal identity, let alone a modern national identity, which is generally associated with the French Revolution and later.

Though not widely understood by modern scholars, Märjani's ideas were extremely important because of the influence they had on the other Muslim Turks of the Russian Empire. By the 1890s the Muslim Turks of the Crimea, who had previously emigrated in great numbers, came to view the Crimea as the ancient home of the Crimean Tatars. The idea of territorial nationalism also spread through various newspapers after 1905, not only among the Tatars of the Middle Volga region but also among Kazakh intellectuals. By 1918 this idea had spread to Khwarezm and Bukhara. This is not to say that the idea of the unity of the Muslim Turks had lost steam completely, since in the Middle Volga region there was a heated debate as to whether they should call themselves Tatars or Turks.

The Rise of Political Movements

The period 1905–1917 was an exciting time for the Muslims of the Russian Empire because of new opportunities for political activity (Muslims were hardly represented in Russian political institutions). On August 15, 1905, the First All-Russian Congress of Muslims was held in Nizhnii Novgorod. The congress had five goals: 1) unification of the Muslims of Russia for the purpose of carrying out political, economic, and social reforms; 2) establishment of a democratic form of government that would allow elected representatives of all nationalities to share in legislative and executive authority; 3) legal equality of Muslims and Russians; 4) freedom to develop Muslim schools, Islamic press and book publishing ventures, and a Muslim cultural life; and 5) periodic meetings of the congress.

The congress was unable to establish a political party, but it did support the concept of a union of all the Muslims of Russia, including a reconciliation of Sunni and Shiite Muslims. The Second All-Russian Congress of Muslims met in St. Petersburg in January 1906 and the Third All-Russian Congress of Muslims met in Nizhnii Novgorod in August 1906. Muslims were able to gain modest representation in the First Russian Duma (1906) and the Second Russian Duma (1907), but they became a weak minority in the Third Russian Duma (1907–1912) and in the Fourth Russian Duma (1912–1917). The arguments made by the Muslim faction (later factions) for political, religious, and cultural equality and increased resources from the state fell on deaf ears. Despite their cooperation with Russian political parties, the Muslims made hardly any gains.

Moreover, the ground was already laid in the First All-Russian Congress of Muslims for the political fragmentation of the Muslims. From the beginning the Muslim congresses could not agree on a unified political program, only on educational and religious issues. Not only did the delegates come from diverse social classes, they represented a wide spectrum of political

A photograph of the Russian parliament, or Duma, which was created after the Russian Revolution of 1905. Although Muslims participated in the Duma, they had little power, and their goal of gaining greater religious and political freedom within the Russian Empire was mostly ignored.

views. There was also the ethnic/regional question: the First All-Russian Congress of Muslims was organized and attended largely by Tatars from the Middle Volga region, although the leadership also included representatives from the Crimea (Gaspirali), Baku (Ali Merdan Toptchibashi), and other regions. Nevertheless, the domination of the congresses by Tatars from the Middle Volga region—who in this period were very active politically—engendered a sense of alienation and political apathy among the Muslims living in other regions of the Russian Empire. The conservative backlash of the Russian authorities in 1907 also led some of the participants in the first Muslim congresses to emigrate to Turkey and elsewhere.

A decade later, but in a new era following the abdication of Tsar Nicholas II, another First All-Russian Congress of Muslims met in Moscow on May 1, 1917, with 800 to 900 delegates from around the Russian Empire. This congress also foundered over the Tatars of the Middle Volga region, but this time the issue was territory. Whereas most of the Tatar delegates from the Middle Volga region favored non-territorial cultural autonomy within a centralized

Russian republic (that is, no separate territorial unit), the representatives from Azerbaijan, the Crimea, and Central Asia favored territorial autonomy with a federal republic. As a result, when the Second All-Russian Congress of Muslims met in Kazan in July and August 1917, there was practically no participation by delegates from Azerbaijan, the Crimea, and Central Asia.

Once again the Muslims of the Russian Empire were fragmenting. The Crimean Tatars had their own congress in March 1917. The Bashkirs also had one in July 1917, agreeing to seek autonomy with the other Turkic tribes of the steppe region and Turkistan. The Kazakhs had a rising sense of regional nationalism as well as the imperative for action in the face of growing territorial losses to agricultural colonists, which led to the establishment of the Alash Orda party in March 1917. The First Pan-Kyrgyz Congress met in Orenburg in April 1917. (In the 19th and early 20th centuries the Russians would refer to the Kazakhs of today as the "Kyrgyz," while they would refer to the Kyrgyz of today as the "Kara Kyrgyz.") This congress called for limited autonomy and the use of the Kazakh language. The Second Pan-Kyrgyz Congress, held in Orenburg in July 1917, supported a Russian state based on federalism. The Alash Orda leaders were for gradually settling the nomadic Kazakhs and were not anti-Russian, while the Kazakhs farther to the south were more nationalistic and anti-Russian. Central Asia had also awakened politically following the rebellion of 1916 sparked by the conscription of Central Asians into worker battalions. The Muslims of Central Asia began meeting in their own congresses in Tashkent in 1917. The peoples of the North Caucasus also met in Vladikavkaz in 1917.

The Muslims of the Middle Volga region would revise their position on autonomy during the National Assembly of the Muslims of Inner Russia and Siberia, which met in Ufa from November 1917 to January 1918. But by then the world had already changed.

ЧИС
ТОТА·

ЗАЛОГ
ЗДО·
РОВЬЯ

A Muslim man stands outside of his stall at a market in the Soviet Union. Although millions of Muslims lived in the USSR, the government officially prevented them from practicing their religion freely.

6

Islam in the USSR

$\mathcal{T}$he life of the Muslims of the Russian Empire would change forever beginning in 1917. Early that year, strikes in Petrograd (the former St. Petersburg) led to the abdication of Tsar Nicholas II, after which the Duma established a provisional government. In November 1917 (October 1917 according to the "Old Style" calendar) the Bolsheviks, led by Vladimir Lenin, seized power during what came to be known as the "October Revolution." Russia signed a peace treaty with Germany to end its participation in World War I, thereby relinquishing control over territories it had annexed earlier, such as Poland, Ukraine, and the Baltic states. The rest of the country disintegrated into a civil war between the "Whites"

This photograph of Bolshevik leaders Vladimir Lenin (left) and Joseph Stalin was taken in 1922, the year the Union of Soviet Socialist Republics (USSR) was formed. After Lenin's death in 1924, Stalin emerged from a struggle for power as the USSR's sole ruler in 1929. Stalin's policies—particularly collectivization of agriculture, repression of the practice of Islam, and forced deportation of ethnic minorities from their homelands to other parts of the Soviet Union—had a terrible effect on the Muslims of the USSR.

(royalists) and "Reds" (Bolsheviks). The Bolsheviks succeeded in regaining full control over the country by late 1922. The first constitution of the Russian Soviet Federated Socialist Republic (RSFSR) was adopted in July 1918. Following the principle of federalism, Lenin reached an agreement with the republics of Ukraine, Belorussia, and Transcaucasia (after the reconquest of the South Caucasus) to establish the Union of Soviet Socialist Republics (USSR). The first constitution of the USSR was adopted in January 1924, shortly after Lenin's death. Lenin was succeeded by Joseph Stalin, whose ruthless policies (including widespread purges during the 1920s and 1930s) would traumatize all peoples of the USSR.

Political and National Reorganization of the Muslims

Very few Muslims were involved in the revolution. The leading figures among the Muslim communities of the Russian Empire were instead engaged in a flurry of congresses and negotiations over the course of 1917. The delegates to the National Assembly of the Muslims of Inner Russia and Siberia (dominated by Tatars from the Middle Volga region), which met in Ufa from November 1917 to January 1918, could not agree on whether to have an autonomous territorial Volga-Ural state or a non-territorial autonomy that would unite all the Turks of Russia. In the end, what they thought mattered very little. The new government, which began to appoint Muslims to positions of responsibility, followed its own agenda, including the brutal suppression in February 1918 of the Kokand government that had declared autonomy.

In the Middle Volga region an attempt to establish an autonomous Tatar-Bashkir Soviet Republic (similar to the concept of a Volga-Ural state) failed, and two autonomous soviet socialist republics (ASSRs)—the Tatar ASSR and the Bashkir ASSR—were established in 1920. By January 1921, a total of five ethnic republics—including the non-Muslim Chuvash, Mari, and Voytak (Udmurt) republics—had been established in the region. Farther to the south, in the Black Sea region, a Crimean ASSR was created in October 1921 as part of the RSFSR. This republic, which was established over the objections of the local Russian population, would serve as the national home for the Crimean Tatars.

Central Asia initially had a Kyrgyz ASSR (corresponding roughly to a larger version of today's Kazakhstan), a Turkistan ASSR, and separate people's socialist republics in Bukhara and Khorezm. The national delimitation of 1924 began the complete reorganization of these units into new republics and autonomous republics that are recognizable today. The first union republic (SSR) was the Uzbek SSR. The Kazakh, Kyrgyz, Tajik, and Turkmen SSRs were created in the new USSR constitution adopted in December 1936. After 1936 there would continue to be significant reorganizations (including the creation of the Karakalpak ASSR within the Uzbek SSR) and territorial transfers as late as the 1960s.

In the South Caucasus, Azerbaijan had originally joined the USSR in 1922 as a part of the republic of Transcaucasia. Transcaucasia was dissolved by the Soviet constitution of 1936, at which time the Azerbaijan SSR was established together with the Armenian SSR and the Georgian SSR. In the North Caucasus a number of autonomous republics existed by 1922, namely the Cherkess (Adyge), Karachayevo-Cherkess, Kabardino-Balkar, Mountain (Gorskaya), and Dagestan autonomous republics. The Soviet constitution of 1936 recognized the Dagestan, Kabardino-Balkar, Chechno-Ingush, and North Ossetian ASSRs.

This massive political and national reorganization of the Muslim peoples of the USSR would have lasting consequences. Traditional categories of ethnic identity and territorial organization were disregarded, and the new boundaries drawn in the 1920s and 1930s often did not follow traditional ethnic boundaries. In some cases even the official names of the new nationalities were changed along with boundaries (for example, the earlier Kyrgyz ASSR formed the basis of the later Kazakh SSR). There were cases in which closely related ethnic groups that could easily have formed one republic were divided into smaller republics. Unrelated peoples were also forced together into new republics. For example, the Tatars and Bashkirs were arguably a single people (or else two closely related ethnic groups), but they were given two separate republics. In another example, separate Karachayevo-Cherkess and Kabardino-Balkar republics were established, even though the Karachays and Balkars are also more or less a single people, while the Kabarda are related to the Cherkess.

Finally, one cannot pass over in silence the severe disruption that was caused by Stalin's deportation of the Muslim Balkars, Chechens, Crimean Tatars, Ingush, Karachays, and Meskhetian Turks (as well as some non-Muslim nationalities living in the same region) in 1943–1944. Roughly 700,000 people were deported to Central Asia and Siberia, the bulk of whom were Chechens and Ingush. Many of the deportees died in railroad cars en route; others suffered greatly from hunger, exposure, and the lack of any support infrastructure whatsoever in their places of exile. To add insult to injury, the deportees also faced strong discrimination in their new internal exile. The deportations also had administrative consequences: the Chechno-Ingush ASSR was dismantled and the Crimean Tatar ASSR was downgraded in status and transferred later to the Ukraine. The lands and homes of the deportees were given over to their neighbors, who in some cases were members of other Muslim groups. When the deported peoples began to be allowed back to their original homelands in 1957, new conflict emerged between them and the Christians and Muslims now occupying their former homes and lands.

Muslim Life in the Soviet Period

The Soviet policy of "official atheism" led to an assault on all forms of religious life, causing a tremendous degradation in religious institutions. Muslims suffered the same as Christians, Jews, and Buddhists. Most mosques and Islamic schools were shut down, though some were maintained as showcases for visiting dignitaries. Mosques that were not physically destroyed were put to other uses (for example, as stables or warehouses). There was also an assault on the members of the religious class as well as on the brotherhoods of the Sufi mystical orders.

The early Soviet policy of national and territorial reengineering led to a redefinition of certain already existing nations (notably the Kazan Tatars) and the formation of new Muslim nationalities (today nations)

Wearing the traditional black-and-white cap known as the *do'ppi*, Uzbek men pray in a mosque in Margelan.

across the territory of the USSR. Because of official atheism, there was a de-Islamization of identity for the former Muslim populations of the Russian Empire, be they Turkic, Iranian, or Caucasian. Henceforth nationalities would be defined culturally and linguistically, not on the basis of religion. Russian was the official language of inter-ethnic communication, so Soviet citizens were required by law to use Russian when in the presence of members of other ethno-linguistic groups. (Of course, the peoples of the North Caucasus spoke so many different languages that Russian was already serving as a language of inter-ethnic communication; literary Arabic had also been used as a common language in early newspapers in the North Caucasus.) Even in Muslim republics, many parents preferred to send their children to Russian-language schools because a Russian-language education offered better professional opportunities across the whole country, not just in their native republic.

In the 1920s there was a separate ideology of Muslim national communism. This idea was associated with Mirsaid Sultangaliev (1880–1939?), a Kazan Tatar who would later become one of the countless victims of Stalin's purges. The supporters of this idea felt that Tatars were a proletarian nation because they had suffered tremendously under Russian colonial occupation. In their view, the Tatars were ready for revolution, but they aspired to a national revolution with greater national autonomy rather than to a socialist revolution. The efforts by this group to "Tatarize" the revolution—understandable given the highly developed national consciousness of the Tatars of the Volga region—and their continuing respect for Islam, which they believed to be compatible with socialism, ultimately led to their undoing. Moscow rejected a separate Muslim path to communism as a national deviation, and Kazan was stripped of its de facto role as a cultural and political center for the Muslims of the USSR. It is largely because of this episode that the Kazan Tatars henceforth had a second-class status in the Soviet Union as an autonomous republic within the Russian Federation (in contrast to the future union republics of Central Asia, for example).

In addition to the assault on the wealthy class and the families of prosperous peasants (maligned as *kulaks*), there was a broad assault on the traditional cultural practices of the non-Russian population. In particular, traditions of the Muslim population that were regarded as "backwards" came under attack by the state, partly because the authorities viewed them as connected with the Islamic religion. The veiling of women (traditionally women in Central Asia only covered their hair in the pre-colonial period), the payment of a dowry or bride-price in concluding marriages, and religious ceremonies during major life cycle events such as birth or death were now strongly discouraged as "crimes of tradition." In Central

Asia there was strong resistance to the establishment of Bolshevik rule; these counterrevolutionary groups are known in English as the *basmachi*.

The Soviet period also saw the introduction of uniform state regulation of Islamic institutions across the USSR, which was organized along these new national principles. There were four Spiritual Boards (*Dukhovnoye upravlenie*) in the USSR:

1. The Spiritual Board of the European Part of the USSR and Siberia, based in Ufa, capital of the Bashkir ASSR of the Russian Federation. Its antecedent was established under Catherine the Great in the late 18th century.

2. The Spiritual Board of the North Caucasus and Dagestan, based in Makhachkala, capital of the Dagestan ASSR of the Russian Federation.

3. The Spiritual Board of Central Asia and Kazakhstan (established in 1946), based in Tashkent, capital of the Uzbek SSR. There were five *qazis* (or "religious judges"), one for each of the five Central Asian union republics. The other Spiritual Boards were later subordinate to the Spiritual Board of Central Asia and Kazakhstan.

4. The Spiritual Board of Transcaucasia, based in Baku, capital of the Azerbaijan SSR. This was the only Spiritual Board that governed Shia religious affairs in addition to Sunni religious affairs of the Hanafi school.

These Spiritual Boards were more for impressing visiting dignitaries from other Muslim countries than for meeting the spiritual needs of the population. The boards appointed, paid, and controlled all *ulema*, or "religious scholars," in the USSR. There were only two functioning madrasas, one in Bukhara and one in Tashkent, which is in sharp contrast to the abundance of Islamic religious colleges during the Imperial period. It has been estimated that in the Soviet era the number of working mosques (supported by local committees with an *imam-xatib,* or prayer leader) may have numbered only about 350 to 450.

The large-scale closure of public Islamic institutions meant that, at least at first, the practice of Islam was forced underground among those Muslims who did not abandon their religion in the cause of building socialism. I would argue that among the masses of Muslims living in the USSR, most Islamic knowledge was lost over the course of the Soviet period. (Certainly I would observe on the basis of my own first-hand knowledge of Kazan Tatars who left the Soviet Union during World War II that knowledge of Islam was already quite weak then.) On the other hand, during the Cold War era some Euro-American scholars of Islam in the USSR, such as Alexandre Bennigsen and S. Enders Wimbush, argued that there was continuity in the activities of Sufi orders. More recently, Ahmed Rashid has assumed that Islamic practice continued unabated in an underground form in the USSR and laid the groundwork for militant Islam in Central Asia today. Upon the collapse of the USSR in 1991, scholars have had tremendous difficulty confirming such claims. Some evidence suggests that in very remote areas such as the Dagestan ASSR in the North Caucasus, there was underground activity of Sufi orders, or that in the Uzbek SSR there was an isolated case of an underground teacher of Islam who remained active. These were the exception rather than the rule. On the whole, we can speak of a radical decline in knowledge of orthodox Islam among the Muslims of the Soviet Union.

The more or less complete reengineering of the Muslim nationalities meant a cultural and religious break with the past in more ways than one. The first sphere in which this was accomplished was education. Whereas the former religious schools had, for example, taught students how to recite the Qur'an in Arabic and how to read other religious and devotional texts in Arabic script in Arabic, Persian, or Turkic languages, clearly this was counter to the purposes of the new communist regime and its anti-religious campaign. Henceforth, outside of the madrasas run by the Spiritual Board of Central Asia and Kazakhstan, the study of Arabic and Islamic sciences would be limited to university faculties of Oriental studies. Traditional Islamic education was replaced by a new system of secular education from primary school through university or other form of higher education. One must acknowledge the great success of this effort at secular education, given the high level of educational achievement by all peoples—including the various Muslim nationalities—during the Soviet period.

The second sphere in which Soviet authorities effected a break with Muslims' cultural and religious past was language. All the Muslim peoples of the Russian Empire used the Arabic script, which often masked the dif-

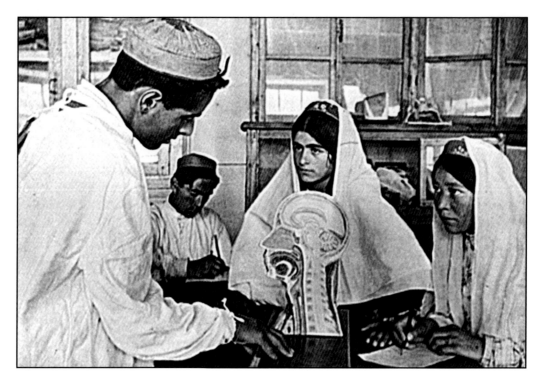

Ethnic Tajik nurses take part in a training course in Khorog, a city in the Kuhistoni Badakhshon region, circa 1938. The Soviet government provided education and health care to all of its citizens, although the quality of these varied widely from region to region.

ferences between the literary and spoken dialects. (The Arabic script had also undergone various orthographic reforms early in the 20th century to make it a more precise tool for accurately rendering the phonetics of the wide range of languages spoken by Muslims.) Nevertheless, in the late 1920s the Turkic languages adopted a unified Latin alphabet (the *Yangälif*), which immediately meant that in the future fewer people would be able to read the earlier literature in Arabic script. Those individuals who knew only Arabic script were suddenly functionally illiterate for all official purposes. Later, in the late 1930s, each of the various Turkic languages adopted a unique Cyrillic-based alphabet. Not only did this new alphabet reform create a second wave of mass functional illiteracy for Muslims, it meant that ordinary speakers of Turkic tongues would no longer be able to read with ease works written in one another's languages, since the individual new literary languages, usually based on strongly divergent dialects, were now written in individual versions of the Cyrillic alphabet with many unfamiliar letters. Among all the nationalities of the USSR, only the Armenians and Georgians—both historically Christian—were spared adopting the Cyrillic alphabet. (Stalin himself was Georgian.)

Literature and the arts constituted the third sphere in which a break with Muslim peoples' past was accomplished. Each new Soviet nationality developed its own tradition of national vernacular literature, folk music, and art under strong Russian cultural influence. Aided by the in-migration of Russians, Kazan Tatars, and others, the republics established new universities, newspapers, publishing houses, orchestras, operas, ballets, and so on. Elements of traditional culture were now used in new ways, following the Soviet dictum of "national in form, socialist in content." The new national cultures were expected to follow officially sanctioned models from the new Soviet Russian culture, such as the novels by Gorky written in Russian. Especially in regions like Central Asia, the Stalinist purges of the late 1920s and 1930s left the ranks of modernizing intellectuals thinned. In most cases

A **Soviet propaganda poster from 1931** encourages farmers to embrace collectivization and gather the harvest for the good of the Soviet state. According to communist ideology, the demands of the state (in this case, the Soviet Union) supersede the needs of individuals. Because organized religions like Orthodox Christianity and Islam posed a potential challenge to the authority of the state, communist leaders attempted to eliminate the practice of religion in the Soviet Union.

this led to the rise of new Soviet-era literatures based heavily on European genres (for example, the short story, novel, and drama), rather than indigenous traditions such as poetry, beginning in the late 1930s. Even though some Muslim modernizers had adopted such new literary models around the turn of the century, the literatures that emerged in the late 1930s now stressed new themes such as the oppressive nature of the earlier wealthier classes ("the bourgeois feudals"), the hardships endured by the poor working classes, and the glorious path of revolution learned from the Russian "older brother."

While the original promise of Lenin was that the different peoples of the former Russian Empire might develop freely, either this promise was a lie or the terms of the promise were altered radically by Stalin. On the eve of World War II (1939–1945), many of the Muslim cultures of the USSR were on a trajectory to being phased out. The USSR's involvement in the war changed that in ways that could not have been anticipated. The surrender of large numbers of Red Army troops and the initial gains of the invading

Germans led the Soviet leadership to relocate many of the country's human and industrial resources to Central Asia and, late in the war, to a campaign to instill a deeper sense of patriotism among all the Soviet peoples through a promotion of pride in the local national cultures. This Soviet campaign to maintain the loyalty of its non-Russian population may have actually saved many of the Muslim cultures of the USSR.

Only in the era of Nikita Khrushchev (1953–1964), who denounced Stalin following his death in 1953, did writers in the USSR, notably the Kyrgyz writer Chingis Aitmatov, dare challenge the traditional Soviet model—often through lyrical stories of love that included a hint of criticism of the history and trajectory of socialism. By the 1960s and 1970s the Muslim peoples of the USSR had assimilated in large measure to Soviet life, though by 1980 Aitmatov would write his famous novel *The Day Lasts More than a Hundred Years*, which introduced the late-Soviet term *Mankurt*, referring to peoples who have lost a knowledge of their own past. (As used in Central Asia and elsewhere, the term now means someone from an indigenous people who has no knowledge of his or her own language or culture. Of course, such a person will never be fully accepted as a Russian, either.) The policy of *korenizatsiya*, or creating national cadres, meant that in most Muslim republics the local Communist Party was at least led by a representative of the local titular nationality. By 1980, however, there were

The writer Chingis Aitmatov (above), an ethnic Kyrgyz, wrote about the loss of identity among the various Muslim peoples of Central Asia.

relatively few people still alive who had received a thorough Islamic education in the pre-Soviet period. Rather, most people had gone through the Soviet educational system by this time.

Thus, by the late 20th century, Islam had become a cultural rather than a strong religious element in the identity of the individual Muslim peoples of the USSR. In the capitals of major Muslim republics such as Kazan in the Tatar ASSR or Almaty in the Kazakh SSR, even knowledge of the language of the titular nationality had declined significantly as parents sent their children to Russian-language schools. In such cities the number of primary schools where students were taught in the local language declined precipitously. Indeed, the late Soviet era saw the rise of a new "Soviet" ethnicity through increasing intermarriage between various nationalities. Today there is great nostalgia for this era under Leonid Brezhnev (1964–1982) and his successors Yuri Andropov (1982–1984) and Konstantin Chernenko (1984–1985).

One could well imagine that the long-term fate of the Muslims of the USSR was assimilation through peaceful means—as opposed to the policies of Stalin (including the imposition of famine on Central Asia and Ukraine, which were widely seen as bordering on genocide). But then Mikhail Gorbachev came along.

The Gorbachev Era

When Mikhail Gorbachev became General Secretary of the Communist Party of the USSR in March 1985, he did not believe that the Soviet Union had a "nationalities problem." He did believe, however, that Soviet society could be strengthened (or perhaps saved?) through *glasnost'* ("openness") and *perestroyka* ("restructuring"). He felt that these two essential reform policies would help Soviet society meet the challenges from the West.

Gorbachev probably did not foresee that his liberal policies would have the most profound consequences for all the nationalities of the

USSR, including the Muslim nationalities. One of the worst problems he inherited was the war in Afghanistan. Following the Soviet invasion of its southern neighbor on December 25, 1979, the USSR became increasingly mired in a bloody war it could not win, especially given the covert aid the United States funneled to the *mujahidin* (Islamic "holy warriors"). Afghanistan became a magnet for Islamists from the Middle East and elsewhere (including Osama bin Laden) who took up arms in support of a Muslim nation invaded by "godless communists." Meanwhile, the war in Afghanistan became increasingly unpopular in the Soviet Union, as returning Russian veterans told their stories and mothers of the fallen organized public protests, taking advantage of Gorbachev's policy of

Mohammed Najibullah (center), head of the puppet Soviet regime in Afghanistan, reviews Red Army troops during a military parade in Kabul, 1986. The Soviet invasion of Afghanistan in 1979 led to a 10-year-long civil war and contributed to an increase in anti-Soviet feeling among Muslims.

glasnost'. The war had serious repercussions in Central Asia as well. At one point the USSR was sending Muslim troops from Central Asia to fight their co-ethnics in Afghanistan. In the Uzbek SSR riots sometimes broke out at the funerals of Uzbek soldiers who had been killed in Afghanistan.

In certain respects, Gorbachev's call for glasnost' opened a Pandora's box of crises and movements that challenged the whole Soviet system. In addition to the Afghan war protests, the Soviet Union experienced, for the first time since the suppression of the *basmachi*, the rise of national movements. The only one that was officially tolerated was the Nevada-Semipalatinsk movement (termed "eco-nationalism") against nuclear testing. It was established following a 1989 speech in Almaty by the Kazakh poet Olzhas Suleymenov.

Otherwise the Muslim regions of the USSR witnessed a series of events—some peaceful, some violent—that foreshadowed the later collapse of the USSR. In December 1986 bloody riots broke out in Almaty after Dinmukhamed Kunayev (an ethnic Kazakh) was replaced as First Secretary of the Communist Party of the Kazakh SSR by Gennadii Kolbin (an ethnic Russian). In mid-1988 meetings were held in the Tatar ASSR that would ultimately lead to the rise of a peaceful grassroots Tatar national movement under the umbrella group known as the Tatar Public Center. In late 1988 the *Birlik* ("Unity") national unity movement was established in the Uzbek SSR. In 1988–1989 a growing crisis developed between the Armenian SSR and the Azerbaijan SSR over the enclave of Nagorno-Karabakh, a part of Azerbaijan at the time. Gorbachev was unable to defuse this crisis (which would escalate into a 1992–1994 war between the independent states of Azerbaijan and Armenia, with the Armenian occupation of Nagorno-Karabakh creating more than a million Azeri refugees). In 1989 disturbances and demonstrations broke out in Tajikistan over land distribution and the use of the Tajik language. That same year an infamous massacre of Meskhetian Turks (who were refugees from the

Caucasus) was carried out by ethnic Uzbeks in Fergana, Uzbek SSR. In 1990 there were riots over land distribution between ethnic Uzbeks and ethnic Kyrgyz in Osh, Kyrgyz SSR.

These movements and disturbances in the Muslim regions of the Soviet Union took place against the backdrop of great political transformations within the USSR. Beginning with the fall of the Berlin Wall in November 1989, the Soviet Empire collapsed as, over the course of the following year, the countries of Eastern Europe declared their independence from Moscow. Recognizing the aspirations of the various peoples of the USSR (including the election of Boris Yeltsin as the first president of the Russian Federation), Gorbachev felt that the time was right for the USSR to conclude a new treaty of union that would loosen the ties between the republics and apparently elevate the Tatar ASSR (whose supreme soviet declared itself the 16th union republic on August 30, 1990) to the status of a union republic.

Shortly before the expected signing of such a treaty, a state of emergency was announced on August 19, 1991. Gorbachev, who was vacationing in the Crimea, was placed under house arrest there while the USSR and the world witnessed an attempted coup in Moscow. The failure of the coup led directly to the outlawing of the Communist Party of the USSR later that same month, and to declarations of sovereignty by the parliaments of each of the union republics. The Minsk Declaration, signed by the presidents of Belarus, Ukraine, and Russia, led to the dissolution of the USSR on December 25, 1991. By coincidence, that was the 12th anniversary of the Soviet invasion of Afghanistan.

The collapse of the USSR made possible the emergence of six new Muslim states (Azerbaijan, Kazakhstan, Kyrgyzstan, Tajikistan, Turkmenistan, and Uzbekistan). The next chapter will focus on the fate of the Muslims in the Russian Federation, the largest of the 15 former union republics.

A Russian soldier aims an automatic rifle at the star and crescent that adorned the top of a destroyed mosque in Grozny, capital of the southern republic of Chechnya.

7

Islam in the Russian Federation

For the second time in a century, the political system of the former Russian Empire changed profoundly and without warning. The sudden collapse of the USSR in 1991 left Boris Yeltsin as the first president of the independent Russian Federation, now one of 15 sovereign successor states to the former USSR. (The 12 union republics—excluding the Baltic republics—now belong to a formal association called the Commonwealth of Independent States, or CIS.)

As in all of the other former union republics, the transition to sovereign state has been difficult in

Russia. Yeltsin was elected president of the RSFSR a short time before the failed putsch of August 1991. That month, the world saw Boris Yeltsin resisting the attempted coup on top of a tank in front of the "Russian White House" (the home of the Soviet-era Congress of People's Deputies and now the home of the Russian Duma). But two years later, in September 1993, the world saw a different picture, as Yeltsin ordered Russian tanks to fire on the same building after deputies resisted his edict dissolving the Soviet-era parliament. Yeltsin had the resisters arrested, and elections were held for a new Duma, or Russian parliament, later the same year. Yeltsin himself was elected to a second term in 1996, but this second term proved a disappointment, especially once his health declined following heart surgery in late 1996. On December 31, 1999, Yeltsin unexpectedly announced his retirement in favor of Prime Minister Vladimir Putin, who was sworn in as acting president. Putin, a former officer in the KGB (the USSR's much-feared state security agency), was elected to his first term as president in March 2000; in March 2004 he won reelection, with his second term scheduled to run through 2008. While Yeltsin's presidency may be characterized as a period of democratization, federalism, and stagnation, Putin's presidency may be seen as a period of centralization and creeping authoritarianism. The same tendencies are reflected in the Russian Federation's policies toward its Muslim population.

Islam in the Russian Federation

Nearly 12.5 million people, or about 8.6 percent of the Russian Federation's total population of more than 145 million, belong to traditionally Muslim ethnic groups, according to the 2002 census. (One frequently encounters unofficial estimates claiming that there are closer to 20 million Muslims in Russia, but this figure is probably exaggerated.) The most important concentrations of Muslims are found in the Middle Volga region, the Urals, Western Siberia, the Lower Volga region, the North

Caucasus, and the cities of Moscow and St. Petersburg. Many Muslims live in former autonomous republics (now simply called "republics") whose titular nationality is Muslim—namely, Bashqortostan and Tatarstan in the north, and Adygeya, Chechnya, Dagestan, Ingushetia, Kabardino-Balkaria, and Karachayevo-Cherkessia in the south. Muslims also live as minorities in other ethnic republics, including Chuvashia, Mari El, Mordovia, Udmurtia, and Northern Ossetia, or in enclaves in various Russian territories or major cities.

Since 1991 there has been a massive expansion of open religious observance in the Russian Federation. The majority of Russians are Orthodox Christians, but space has also been created for Russia's Muslims and the predominantly Muslim republics to embrace Islam once again. Although it was repressed during the Soviet period, Islam remains an inseparable part of the history and cultural identity of all the modern Muslim nationalities of the Russian Federation. Surprisingly, a growing number of ethnic Russians are also converting to Islam.

In recent years the Russian Federation has witnessed a proliferation of functioning mosques (which numbered only perhaps 350 to 450 during the Soviet era). By 1998 there were more than 5,500 registered mosques in Russia, with about 2,000 in Chechnya, 1,670 in Dagestan, 1,000 in Tatarstan, and 400 in Ingushetia. Today one encounters an unofficial figure of more than 8,000 mosques, which seems entirely reasonable (and is still substantially fewer than existed in Russia in the pre-Soviet period). The number of mosques is likely to continue growing. As of 2005, there were 11 new mosques under construction in Moscow alone, which would raise to 15 the number of Islamic houses of worship in that city. But even that seems inadequate, considering the large number of Muslim refugees from the Caucasus and other regions now living in Moscow, alongside the city's centuries-old Tatar community, which consists of hundreds of thousands of individuals.

The number of Islamic educational institutions in Russia has also increased. By 1998 there were 106 religious schools and 51 registered religious centers and societies providing a basic Islamic education. In Dagestan alone there were 25 madrasas, 670 Islamic primary schools, several "Islamic universities," and numerous other Islamic institutes and educational institutions. Remarkably, almost one-fifth of the population of Dagestan was receiving some sort of Islamic education. In 2000 the Shaykh Muhammad Arif North Caucasian Islamic University was founded in Makhachkala, Dagestan. While this university enrolls students from around the Russian Federation, it is not clear whether any of the Islamic universities in Dagestan have been "officially registered" (accredited) by federal authorities.

Since the collapse of the Soviet Union, Islamic educational institutions have sprung up across Russia. Pictured are the Moscow Cathedral Mosque (left) and the Moscow Islamic University.

Although the number of Islamic educational institutions in Tatarstan cannot compare with the total in Dagestan, there is nonetheless both official and popular interest in promoting Islamic education throughout the Volga region. In 1998 the Russian Islamic University was established in Kazan with the active support of the government of Tatarstan. At the time of its opening it was considered the only officially registered Muslim institution of higher learning in Russia. The university accepts young men between the ages of 17 and 35 who have completed an Islamic secondary school (there is also a preparatory division). The students, who are prospective imams, study Arabic language, the Qur'an and Qur'anic sciences, and Islamic law. The school maintains contacts with similar educational institutions in the CIS countries, and its students have also studied abroad in Jordan and Egypt. More recently, an officially registered Islamic university has opened in Moscow as well.

Also deserving mention are the large number of Turkish secondary schools established throughout the Russian Federation. While they offer an excellent secular education taught in English, the schools are sponsored by a grassroots movement of Turkish businessmen who are followers of the exiled Turkish spiritual leader Fethullah Gülen. Since the FSB (the successor to the KGB) has accused Gülen of working for the U.S. Central Intelligence Agency, it is understandable that these schools are seen as controversial. In August 2002 authorities in Bashqortostan issued a warrant seeking the deportation of three teachers who are Turkish citizens; the warrant alleged that the teachers had engaged in actions contrary to Russia's national interests, including teaching a radical version of Islam. (Considering that Fethullah Gülen's teachings are heavily infused with Islamic mysticism and are the opposite of what Islamic teachers influenced by **Wahhabism** might advocate, such accusations may reflect the authorities' ignorance of the different kinds of Islam.) Nevertheless, these schools continue to enjoy strong support from the population, even from non-Muslim Russian parents who send their children to the schools.

In Soviet times there was no state-sanctioned need for a large number of religious officials. With the proliferation of mosques after 1991, however, there has been a tremendous rise in the number of imams, along with the establishment of a position of mufti (a scholar who interprets Islamic law) in each republic with a significant Muslim population. Thus in the Volga region Tatarstan and Bashqortostan have their own muftis, as do Chuvashia, Mordovia, and Udmurtia (predominantly Christian republics with a significant Muslim minority). Astrakhan, Chelyabinsk, Nizhnii Novgorod, Orenburg, Penza, Perm, Primorskii kray, Rostov region, Samara, Simbirsk (Ulyanovsk), Sverdlovsk, Tyumen, Volgograd, and practically all other political-administrative units have their own muftis in charge of their Muslim minorities (mostly Kazan Tatars). Muslim communities (*mahalla*) are also administered by the regional muftiates, though there is often confusion (or competition) over jurisdiction.

In the North Caucasus each of the six Muslim republics also has its own mufti, as does Northern Ossetia (a predominantly Christian republic with a significant Muslim minority). The muftis in the North Caucasus work in a highly politicized environment because of the conflict in the region. Generally they have remained loyal to the governments of their republics and have opposed the spread of "Wahhabism," which in post-Soviet lingo refers to the Islamist "Arab" fighters who carried their jihad from Afghanistan via Central Asia to the North Caucasus and beyond. In reality, in the post-Soviet context this term is also a code word for any Islamic movement not approved by the local government. While the muftis of the North Caucasus originally participated in the Higher Coordinating Center of Spiritual Boards of the Muslims of Russia, they withdrew from this organization in 1998 and formed a separate Coordinating Center of Muslims of the North

Caucasus, which then sought to improve ties with its counterparts in the South Caucasus.

The all-Russian institutional organization of the Muslims of the Russian Federation has been undergoing a controversial transformation since the collapse of the USSR and the end of the state doctrine of official atheism. Since 1991 four notable trends have emerged: the infusion of financial support for Islam in Russia from domestic and especially foreign sources; the struggle over which old or new institutions will have supremacy over the Muslims of Russia; the "nationalization" of religious institutions; and the intrusion of ethnic politics into religious affairs.

With religion no longer outlawed in the Russian Federation, it has been possible for individuals, communities, companies, and even local governments to support Muslim religious institutions in one form or another. As the wealth of individual businessmen has increased, they have also become influential patrons of religious institutions and schools (especially among Muslims in Siberia). Particularly noteworthy is the foreign aid that has flowed to Russian Muslim institutions from Muslim countries, especially Saudi Arabia, Kuwait, and the United Arab Emirates, as well as from a variety of international Islamic organizations, charities, and universities. This money has been used to support participation by Russian Muslims in the hajj, study by Russian Muslims at Islamic universities and colleges in a variety of countries, the building of mosques, and the publishing and distribution of Islamic religious literature.

It should be noted that aid from Saudi Arabia is usually associated with the propagation of Wahhabism, the dominant Islamic sect in Saudi Arabia today. This puritanical, intolerant understanding of Islam emerged in Arabia in the 18th century as a rejection of Sufism and other supposed "innovations" in the practice of Islam (innovation in the religion is considered to be anti-Islamic). Imams returning home after training in Saudi

Russia's prime minister, Mikhail Kasyanov, welcomes Saudi Arabia's Crown Prince Abdullah to Moscow, September 2003. Over the past decade, Saudi Arabia and other wealthy Arab states of the Persian Gulf have provided financial aid to Russian Muslims.

Arabia often come into conflict with their native communities because of the influence of Wahhabism, which rejects many of the local cultural aspects of Islamic observance among the different communities of Russian Muslims. The revival of Sufism in the North Caucasus and the concept of Tatar Islam as a liberal and tolerant "Euro-Islam" in the Middle Volga region are anathema to imams and other Muslims who have fallen under the influence of Wahhabism.

It will be recalled that during the Soviet period there were four separate regional Spiritual Boards, with the Spiritual Board of Central Asia and Kazakhstan having supremacy. With the independence of the republics of Central Asia and the South Caucasus, only the Spiritual Board of the European Part of the USSR and Siberia (based in Ufa, Bashqortostan) and the Spiritual Board of the North Caucasus and Dagestan (based in Makhachkala, Dagestan) remained on the territory of Russia. After 1991 these two Spiritual Boards struggled to retain their authority (to the extent that they ever had any real authority). In 1994 the Spiritual Board of the European Part of the USSR and Siberia was renamed the Central Spiritual Board of Russia and the CIS, and its leader, Talgat Tajetdin (also spelled Tajuddin or Tadjuddin), became the Supreme Mufti.

The supremacy of the Central Spiritual Board of Russia and the CIS and Supreme Mufti Tajetdin began to be challenged by competing new Spiritual Boards. The two earlier Spiritual Boards were seen as compromised because of their affiliation with the Soviet state and because they continued to be led by the same leaders as in Soviet times. Even worse, there were allegations of corruption against their leaders, especially Tajetdin in Ufa, who was accused of misappropriating a portion of the aid that was flowing in from Islamic countries. In 1992 a group of imams who sought to transfer the Central Spiritual Board of Russia and the CIS from Ufa to Kazan established the Higher Coordinating Center of Spiritual Boards of the Muslims of Russia, which later ceased to be active. A number of positions as regional mufti were also established—such as Mufti of European Russia, Mufti of Asian Russia, Mufti of the Volga Region, and Mufti of Siberia and the Far East—and filled by former associates of Tajetdin. The Mufti of European Russia, Ravil Gainutdin (a Kazan Tatar), is now also chairman of the Moscow-based Council of Muftis of Russia; he is seen as a competitor of Tajetdin for supremacy over the Muslim communities in the Russian Federation. This struggle can be interpreted as a campaign against

President Vladimir Putin meets with Talgat Tajetdin, Supreme Mufti of the Central Spiritual Board of Russia and the CIS, in Ufa, Bashqortostan.

corruption, but it can also be seen as an effort to gain control over the lucrative funding of Islamic institutions in the Russian Federation (including the substantial foreign aid from Islamic countries). The competition between Ufa and Kazan taps into the traditional Soviet-era nationalist rivalry between Bashqortostan and Tatarstan. The centralization of Islamic institutions in Moscow is also consistent with the process of centralization taking place in other areas of Russian political life.

The Politics of Islam in the Russian Federation

With the sudden collapse of the USSR, the Russian Federation faced a series of issues nobody was prepared to deal with: religion, nationalism, transition to a market economy, and especially separatism. Under the former Russian Empire, there were no national territorial units, which were created only in the Soviet era. The national awakening that took place in the USSR during the Gorbachev era had its resonances in the RSFSR as well. Beginning in the 1980s there were renewed calls for greater autonomy for the Tatar ASSR by Tatars concerned for the fate of Tatar language and culture. After 1991 Tatarstan continued to press for sovereignty, while Chechnya pressed for complete independence. The tale of these two republics—especially the tragedy of Chechnya—is instructive for understanding the politics of Islam in the Russian Federation.

As noted in the previous chapter, on the eve of the failed coup that led to the collapse of the USSR, there was a real hope that the Tatar ASSR would finally attain the status of union republic (an issue first raised in 1936). After all, Kazan Tatars had a long history of compact settlement, a national state tradition, and the other requirements imposed by the USSR Constitution for achieving the status of union republic. Had it been a union republic at the time of the coup, Tatarstan might have become an independent state in 1991, but the chances were slim that the newly independent Russian Federation would ever willingly grant Tatarstan independence.

The call for increased rights for Tatarstan did not disappear, however. Kazan Tatars had a highly developed intelligentsia with a strong sense of national identity. Soviet policies promoting a cultural and linguistic decline in Tatarstan, combined with the fact that most Tatars outside of Tatarstan had no cultural support, had led to a grassroots movement to save Tatar language and culture in the Gorbachev era. On June 13, 1991, voters in Tatarstan voted for president of Tatarstan rather than for president of Russia, an act symbolizing their belief in the sovereignty of the republic.

In order to create a basis in international law for its position, on March 21, 1992, Tatarstan held a referendum. A majority of eligible voters in Tatarstan (including ethnic Russians) voted in favor of the proposition that the republic of Tatarstan is a sovereign state (affirming the earlier declaration of August 30, 1990). Russian political figures anticipated bloodshed in the streets (and insiders say that Tatarstan was surrounded by Russian tanks at this time), but the referendum was conducted peacefully.

Tatarstan was one of two republics that refused to sign the new Treaty of Federation in 1992, insisting instead on negotiations with Yeltsin's government. (Insiders say that Tatarstan demanded to see the documents incorporating the Tatar ASSR into the RSFSR in the first place, but that the Russian side could never produce such documents.) Following lengthy negotiations in 1994, the Russian Federation finally consented to a series of power-sharing agreements with Tatarstan in which Tatarstan would be a state united with Russia on the basis of the constitutions of the two states and the new treaty. Whereas the Russian Federation would be responsible for foreign affairs, customs, currency, and the like, Tatarstan would have a certain degree of responsibility for domestic affairs on the basis of revenue-sharing and cooperation with the federal authorities. Most important, the agreements created an official space to promote Tatar language and culture, including Islam. This new arrangement, which would henceforth be known as the "Tatarstan model," was widely lauded internationally as a model of federalism. Following Tatarstan's lead, by late 1995 Bashqortostan, Karachayevo-Cherkessia, Kabardino-Balkaria, Sakha (Yakutia), and Buryatia had signed similar agreements. Later other political-administrative units sought or signed power-sharing agreements with the federal center. Needless to say, this created a complicated political situation for Moscow.

Recently, the Russian government has sought to backtrack on those arrangements in negotiations on the renewal of the power-sharing agreements. Although the government of the Russian Federation is not a monolith, since Putin became president there has been a steady strengthening and centralization of federal institutions. In a move seen as undermining the status of the regional governors and presidents of republics, in May 2000 Putin divided the Russian Federation into seven regional districts and decreed that the regional administrators in charge of these districts would henceforth serve as his personal representatives to the republics and regions. This new bureaucratic layer has not been viewed universally as a successful move by Putin. Most recently, in December 2004 Putin signed a law giving the president the right to appoint Russia's 89 regional leaders. These appointees must be confirmed by the regional legislatures, but if the Russian president's nominee is rejected twice, the Russian president can dissolve the regional legislature and appoint an acting governor of his own choice. This was a tremendous setback for democracy, federalism, and the ethnic republics, since it eliminated the direct election of presidents by the local population.

From the perspective of Tatarstan, Moscow's policies are seen as a continuous low-intensity assault on the republic and its ability to serve the needs of the Tatar nation. In the realm of education, the federal center has taken over the responsibility for registering universities (making it difficult to open a new national university), determining the number of hours of instruction for subjects in primary and secondary schools (reducing the number of hours of Tatar language classes), and approving the content of primary and secondary textbooks (making it difficult to have textbooks that do not follow Russian national history in portraying Tatars in a negative light). Moscow has also presided over the centralization of national radio and television networks, making it more difficult to have local programming in Tatarstan; it has also ended the local retransmission of programs broadcast on shortwave frequencies by the Tatar-Bashkir Service of U.S.-sponsored Radio Liberty. Such steps give the strong impression that the federal authorities are trying to make it ever more difficult for Tatarstan to promote its own language and culture—not to mention the fact that Moscow has moved to claim oil revenues from the republic.

Kazan Tatars were also upset at what they saw as efforts to classify Tatars into subgroups in the October 2002 census, believing this was an attempt to undercount Tatars and divide up the nation. Even most of the minority Kräshen Tatars, who are Christians (they were forcibly converted in waves following the conquest of the Khanate of Kazan in 1552) identified themselves as Kazan Tatars in the census. This represented a failure for the Russian state as well as for the Orthodox Church, which was trying to separate the Kräshen Tatars (who are indistinguishable from the Muslim Kazan Tatars except by their personal names and religion) from the majority Kazan Tatars. More recently, in November 2004, the Russian Constitutional Court upheld legislation from 2002 outlawing the use of any alphabet other than the Cyrillic by the peoples of the Russian Federation. This was a direct response to calls in Tatarstan to substitute the Latin alphabet for the Cyrillic alphabet used by Russian. (The ruling affects not only Tatars, however; Karelians, whose language is related to Finnish, have protested that the ruling will destroy their language.) There is no question that these efforts to promote centralization over federalism serve to strengthen Russian and Orthodox Christian interests at the expense of Tatar and Muslim interests. Nevertheless, Tatars have persisted quietly in trying to make the system work in their favor to the extent possible. The fate of Chechnya suggests the disaster that Tatarstan has been able to avoid.

The origin of the Chechen conflict goes back to 1989, when Chechen nationalists led by the former major general Dzhokhar Dudayev sought the status of union republic for the Chechens. Later, Chechno-Ingushetia and all other republics followed Tatarstan in declaring sovereignty. In October 1991 the All-National Congress of the Chechen People declared a separate Chechnya to be an independent country, with Dudayev as its president. The next year, Chechnya joined Tatarstan in refusing to sign the Treaty of Federation. Rather than seeking a peaceful compromise similar to the one reached with Tatarstan, however, the Russian government sent troops into

Chechnya in December 1994. The leaders of the other republics in the North Caucasus and the Volga region were strongly critical of this move, though President Shaymiyev of Tatarstan also criticized Dudayev for not concluding a similar power-sharing agreement with Moscow. Fighting was suspended in May 1996 as a result of the Khasavyurt Accord. A year later Yeltsin and Chechen president Aslan Maskhadov (who was elected after the assassination of Dudayev in 1996) signed a cease-fire agreement. This did not, however, resolve the status of Chechnya.

Clearly, the course taken by Chechnya was more confrontational than that taken by Tatarstan. Nevertheless, one can argue that the war in Chechnya was unnecessary. What is indisputable is that the results were tragic—for the Chechen people, for the Russians living in Chechnya, and for the Russian soldiers serving in Chechnya. According to one estimate, 90,000 people—including 40,000 civilians and 7,000 Russian soldiers—lost their lives. The city of Grozny and the infrastructure of the republic

Chechen soldiers prepare for an attack by Russian armored vehicles in a trench outside Grozny, December 1994.

were severely damaged and the oil industry was destroyed (a major pipeline passed through Grozny). The situation led to the rise of new criminal gangs of Chechens and Russians alike. In addition, hundreds of thousands of people became refugees in neighboring republics and as far away as Moscow and Tatarstan. In addition to the many other problems it generated, the war turned the North Caucasus into a zone of instability.

The war in Chechnya has also had profound consequences for Islam in Chechen society. Historically the role of Sufi orders has been very important throughout the North Caucasus, including both Dagestan and Chechnya. Although Wahhabism already enjoyed both intellectual and popular support in Dagestan, the conflict in Chechnya led to the spread of Wahhabism in Chechnya in the second half of the 1990s. Arabs and Islamists from many other countries joined the Chechen war for independence against the Russians, and through them Wahhabism came to be seen as the faith of those who supported the jihad against the Russian infidels. For ordinary Chechen fighters, Wahhabism was connected with the rules of Islamic religious law, the Wahhabi dress code (including specific hair and beard styles), and the rejection of Sufism. The ideology of the Wahhabi movement proved capable of overcoming the differences among the various Chechen tribes (*taip*). Thus, although Chechen society became deeply divided between those who supported the traditional Sufi orders (*tariqat*) and those who supported the Wahhabis, Wahhabism served increasingly as a new unifying ideology.

The incursion into Dagestan by Chechen warlord Shamil Basayev in August to September 1999 (which, it has been alleged, was at the behest of a leading Russian oligarch) resulted in Russia's launching a second war on Chechnya in October 1999. This led to a split in the Chechen leadership: President Maskhadov moved strongly into the Wahhabi camp, while the Chief Mufti of Chechnya, Akhmad Kadyrov, continued to see Wahhabism as a worse evil than Moscow. The timing of these events has been called into question. Putin, a previously obscure figure in Russian national politics, had been appointed prime minister of the Russian Federation only in August. By the end of the year he had become acting president, and he would soon begin campaigning for the presidency. During his now-infamous election campaign, Putin cynically exploited his tough stance against the "Chechen terrorists." It worked: he was elected president in March 2000. Since then, Putin has offered only military solutions to the Chechnya problem, and each year the situation grows worse.

There are widespread reports of lax discipline among the Russian forces, and lawlessness and corruption in Chechnya appear rampant. Over the course of the two Chechen wars, the officer corps of the Russian military has profited from corruption (including the kidnapping of Russian soldiers for ransom in cooperation with local Chechen mafias). By now, one can question whether the civilian administration of Russia has lost effective control of its military in Chechnya. At the same time, the war has taken a terrible toll on the Chechen civilian population. In addition to facing all the dangers of life in a combat zone, Chechen civilians have been subject to abuses such as arbitrary arrest, kidnapping, and "disappearance." Genocide may not be too strong a word to use in describing the state-sponsored destruction of the Chechen people.

Tragically, the March 2005 assassination of former president Maskhadov by Russian special forces may have silenced the last influential Chechen voice who could have worked to settle the conflict. Maskhadov, who was by then an underground separatist leader, had called for peace negotiations in February 2005. In May of the previous year, Maskhadov's former rival, Akhmad Kadyrov, had himself been assassinated while serving as the pro-Russian president of Chechnya. In the near term, prospects for peace in Chechnya appear dim, and some observers worry that the unrest there might trigger a wider conflict throughout the North Caucasus.

Today, Muslims in the Russian Federation are under pressure not just in conservative areas like the North Caucasus, but also in liberal areas like Tatarstan. In most cases, frictions stem not from religious differences per se, but from the fact that Muslims belong to national minorities whose very existence is perceived (rightly or wrongly) as a threat to the unity and territorial integrity of the Russian Federation. A violent wave of Russian ultra-nationalism has been noted in recent years, especially in Moscow, which is now home to large numbers of refugees from the Caucasus. Caucasians in Moscow are regularly subjected to beatings as well as intense police scrutiny (especially since the bloody Chechen attacks on a

Former Chechen president Aslan Maskhadov (right) is pictured with other Chechen rebel leaders in their mountain camp. Maskhadov's assassination in March 2005, many observers worried, might prolong the bloody conflict in Chechnya.

theater in Moscow in October 2002 and the attack on an elementary school in Beslan, North Ossetia, in September 2004).

The policies of the Russian Federation toward the national homelands of its own Muslim citizens—particularly since the rise of Vladimir Putin— have not been particularly enlightened. The government of the Russian Federation has conveniently forgotten the concept of federalism while trying to centralize state authority and downgrade the status of the republics (especially Tatarstan). Other voices in the government see a power-sharing agreement with Chechnya along the lines of the "Tatarstan model" as the only hope for resolving a seemingly insoluble conflict.

A Russian Muslim prepares to slaughter a sheep to mark the first day of the Islamic festival Id al-Adha (Qurban Bayram). This three-day festival commemorates the patriarch Abraham's willingness to sacrifice his son to God.

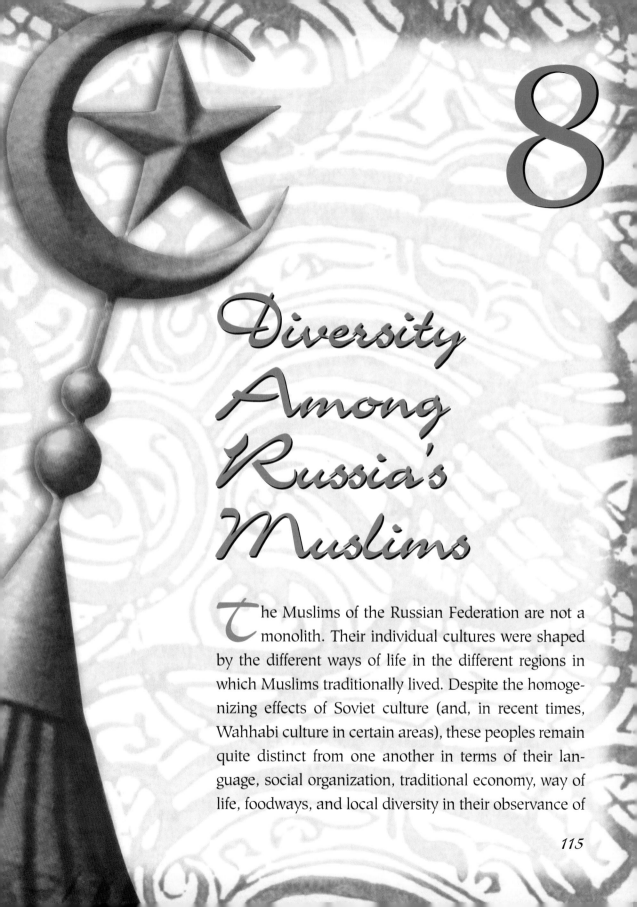

8

Diversity Among Russia's Muslims

The Muslims of the Russian Federation are not a monolith. Their individual cultures were shaped by the different ways of life in the different regions in which Muslims traditionally lived. Despite the homogenizing effects of Soviet culture (and, in recent times, Wahhabi culture in certain areas), these peoples remain quite distinct from one another in terms of their language, social organization, traditional economy, way of life, foodways, and local diversity in their observance of

Islam. Now that the five republics of Central Asia and Azerbaijan in the South Caucasus are independent states, the remaining traditional concentrations of Muslims in the Russian Federation are in the Middle Volga region and the North Caucasus. There is a significant concentration of Muslims in major cities such as Moscow and St. Petersburg, but—except for the traditional Kazan Tatar populations in these cities—most are refugees from the Caucasus and Central Asia. There are also smaller populations in places in the Russian Federation such as Siberia and along the Lower Volga region, which is really a periphery of Central Asia.

One of the largest concentrations of Muslims is in the Middle Volga region, which is home to the Kazan Tatars and the Bashkirs (Bashqort), two very closely related peoples. Based on the 2002 census, these two ethnic groups, counted together, total 7,232,000—57.9 percent of the Muslims of the Russian Federation. (This figure includes the small minority of Kräshen Tatars.) Kazan Tatars live in Tatarstan; Bashqortostan (where they represent the largest single ethnic group); the neighboring republics of Chuvashia, Mari El, Udmurtia, and Mordovia; around cities along the Volga River, such as Simbirsk and Astrakhan; in Perm; and in cities in Siberia such as Chelyabinsk. There is also a strong Tatar diaspora throughout the territories of the former USSR. The Bashkirs live in Bashqortostan.

For reasons of nationalism, the question of the relationship between the Kazan Tatars and the Bashkirs became highly politicized in the 20th century. In brief, the Kazan Tatars of today are descended from the Volga Bulgarians and other Turkic and non-Turkic peoples of the Middle Volga region. In the Golden Horde period and later, there was a very strong influx of Kipchak Turkic peoples, and the modern Kazan Tatar language is a Kipchak Turkic dialect. The Bashkirs, who live to the east of the Kazan Tatars, are also descended from various Turkic and non-Turkic peoples of the Volga-Ural region and were very strongly influenced by Kipchak Turkic

A Tatar woman fetches water from the village well, Tatarstan. Historically, the Tatars of the Volga region have lived in farming communities.

peoples. Bashkir national history relies on the fact that the 10th-century traveler Ibn Fadlan mentions the Bashghird as a separate people, but it is not necessarily clear that these were a Turkic-speaking people. (It has been argued based on other sources that the Bashghird in the medieval sources may have been Hungarian speaking.) Bashkirs used literary Tatar in the pre-Soviet period. The modern Soviet Kazan Tatar and Bashkir literary languages are practically two different dialect versions of the same language, and there is a continuum from Kazan Tatar dialects to Bashkir dialects (as there would be from Austria through Germany to Switzerland). In other words, it is not clear whether the ancestors of the Tatars and Bashkirs were very different from each other and have become closer over the past millennium, or whether they were very similar a thousand years ago and have drifted apart a bit over the past millennium. The sharp break between the two peoples is a function of nationalism and politics in the early 20th century. Otherwise their cultures are very similar.

The Tatars of the Volga region have largely been settled agriculturalists over the past millennium, while the Bashkirs had a strong nomadic tradition until the 19th century. One way to understand the difference between these two peoples is to recognize that a certain tribal system was introduced into the Volga region during the period of the Golden Horde and the Khanate of Kazan, similar to the tribal system of the other khanates of the 15th to 18th centuries. The names of the tribes in the areas inhabited by the Tatars of the Volga region differed from those of the tribes in the areas inhabited by Bashkirs. While Tatars had lost knowledge of their tribal origins by the modern period, Bashkirs still had that knowledge in the early 20th century.

The continental climate of the Volga-Ural region produces four distinct seasons, and the peoples of the region had to prepare throughout the year so that their animals would have enough to eat during the long harsh winter. Because of the nomadic component in their ancestry, these peoples had a strong tradition of animal husbandry, especially sheep and horses. In this region there was a heavy reliance on dairy products, including soft cheese curds and yogurt. There was also a very strong horse culture, probably going back to before the Common Era. Tatars and Bashkirs enjoyed horsemeat as much as they enjoyed kumiss (*qimiz*), which is mildly alcoholic fermented mare's milk (also valued as a cure for tuberculosis). Traditionally other bounties of the northern regions included honey (which could also be used to brew fermented beverages) and fruit that grew locally, such as apples and cherries. In addition to growing hay for their animals, the population also cultivated grains suited for cold climates, such as rye, barley, and oats. During a bad growing season, rye grows a poisonous mold called ergot, and this region was traditionally the area of the world with the leading number of incidents of

Tatars pray in a newly established mosque.

ergotism (a disease that causes psychosis and the loss of limbs). In more modern times ergotism has been eliminated, while the production of wheat, potatoes, and other staples has increased. Tatars traditionally made many different pastry dishes from dough filled with meat or vegetables and baked, fried, or cooked in broth.

Among the Tatars and Bashkirs—as with the other Kipchak Turkic peoples—parents arranged marriages for their sons only with girls from families to whom they were not related in the paternal line going back seven or more generations. Often two tribes regularly exchanged brides. As Tatars became sedentary, this turned into the practice of **exogamy**, with families arranging for a marriage for their son with a family from another village. The traditional way to meet the inhabitants of other villages was at the annual early summer festival (*jiyin*) held in turn by a series of villages. Each village also had its own early summer festival called *Saban tuy*, which is now celebrated as a kind of national holiday at various dates in early summer, depending upon locality. There were numerous other traditional local customs in Tatar villages related to the annual agricultural cycle.

The traditional religion of the peoples of the Volga-Ural region before Islam was shamanism—a belief in spirits of dead ancestors, places (such as groves of trees or bodies of water), natural phenomena, and so on, with a holy man called a shaman acting as the intercessor between this world and the other world. Traces of this period are found in the shapes of older village burials as well as in the house and water spirits that survive in folklore. Otherwise Islam, which has been practiced in the Volga region for more than a millennium, has had a profound effect on local religious observances. The most important religious observances were the major Islamic holidays (the feast at the end of the month of Ramazan and *Qurban Bayram*, the Feast of the Sacrifice). Because of the influence of Sufi orders, especially the Naqshbandi, there was also a strong tradition of celebrating the birthday of the prophet Muhammad by reciting the story of his birth (*mawlid*). Other observances with a strong religious component included funerary practices and the observance of prayers and a feast held 3 days, 7 days, 40 days, and one year after the death of a relative. Among the foods served were traditional Tatar dishes, but one wonders whether the inclusion of rice-based dishes in such feasts has a connection with the Central Asian influences on Tatar Islam, either in the earliest period of conversion or through the later influences of the Naqshbandi Sufi order. Friday is the Muslim holy day, but some Tatars would take ritual baths and read special prayers on Thursday evenings. Friday would also be a day for special meals. (The idea that "there should be the smell of oil frying" is no doubt connected with pre-Islamic ideas of feeding the spirits.) Some of these practices characteristic of Tatar Islam were no doubt the result of Sufi influence. Many aspects of Sufi Islam, such as the visitation of shrines, were rejected in the pre-Soviet era by the modernizing reformers, as well as by those who were influenced by the Salafis (Wahhabis).

Tatars, along with Armenians and Jews, also formed an important merchant diaspora. That is one of the reasons why Tatars could be found all over the former Russian Empire. Of course, in Soviet times there were many other reasons for the internal migration of Tatars from the Volga region. The Tatars of Moscow, St. Petersburg, and other cities are largely drawn from the Tatar populations of the Volga region and nearby regions, so they are quite similar in culture and religious practices. The Tatars of Siberia, however, are a rather different case. While there is a substantial Tatar diaspora from the Volga region in Siberia, there is also the aboriginal "Tatar" population along the major river systems: the Tomsk Tatars, the Baraba Tatars, and the Tobol-Irtysh Tatars. In addition to these groups, there are literally hundreds of smaller *tugum* (descent groups), such as Kuyan (Rabbit) and Torna (Crane). Obviously the word *Tatar* is used more as a catchall name for all the local ethnicities. At the same time, there has been a strong assimilation of large groups of aboriginal Tatars into the larger Kazan Tatar national ethnicity, including through intermarriage. The various Siberian Tatars exhibit a strong retention of pre-Islamic religion such as the belief in various spirits.

If we go south along the Volga region we encounter a large community of Kazakhs in the Saratov region. The Kazakhs were the nomads par excellence of the Eurasian steppe in the modern era. The Kazakhs are also a Kipchak Turkic people. For this reason many aspects of their traditional culture have the same roots as those of the other Kipchak Turkic peoples of the Russian Federation (Kazan Tatars, Bashkirs, Nogays, Karachay-Balkars, Kumyks, and others). Most Kazakhs were nomads until the beginning of the 20th century, however. Therefore Kazakhs still have a very strong sense of their tribal and clan identity. Although Kazakhs adopted many Russian foodways during the Soviet era (which is true of all

The nomadic Kazakhs traditionally lived in round tents, known as yurts; today, some Kazakh herdsmen still live in yurts for part of the year while their livestock herds graze on the steppe.

peoples of the former USSR), even today they retain many aspects of their traditional diet, consuming dairy products (including the dried curd known as *qurt*), horse sausage, and dishes such as fritters (*baursaq*) and boiled meat with broad noodles (*beshbarmaq*).

Kazakh traditions such as dressing newborn infants as dogs to ward off evil spirits and countless other practices documented in the 20th century are a very valuable record of the earlier culture of the nomadic Kipchak Turks, all the more so given the fact that most of these practices have disappeared among the sedentary peoples (except for occasional expressions that have survived). More than the sedentary peoples, the Kazakhs were traditionally viewed as superficially Islamized, though in the late 19th and early 20th centuries the Tatar madrasas included many Kazakhs among their students.

The other main ethnic groups in Central Asia—the Uzbeks, Kyrgyz, Turkmen, and Tajiks—are generally present only as Soviet-era migrants or post-1991 refugees. The Kyrgyz are culturally very close to the Kazakhs. Another group, the Karakalpaks—who have a separate republic within Uzbekistan—are almost indistinguishable from Kazakhs. The Uzbeks are closely related to the Turkic-speaking Uygurs of the People's Republic of China as well as to the Tajiks, who speak a form of Persian called Tajik. (The Uzbeks and Uygurs speak a Turkic language belonging to another group, the Turki group, which is also known by other names.) The Uzbeks, Uygurs, and Tajiks all developed oasis cultures in a rather hot and arid zone. The popular Islam in Uzbekistan and Tajikistan reveals the strong influence of earlier Iranian religions such as Zoroastrianism, including cultural references to the importance of fire. The Turkmen—who belong to the Oghuz group of the Turkic peoples, together with the Azerbaijanis and Turks of Turkey—live in an even drier region along the Iranian border. Although they have been Muslim for a millennium, their popular religion is heavily infused with pre-Islamic and Sufi traditions popular in all of Central Asia, including the visitation of shrines for blessings and cures. In post-Soviet times there has been a revival of the ancient Iranian New Year holiday known as Navruz, which is now celebrated throughout Central Asia as a national holiday. Although this holiday is less well known in places like the Volga region or in Turkey (where it was only celebrated by Kurds), it is growing in public recognition in Tatarstan and Turkey, too.

The North Caucasus is a very complex amalgam of different Muslim peoples, some of whom converted to Islam only in the last several centuries. Some belong to Turkic peoples who formerly roamed vast portions of the Eurasian steppe; others are descended from the ancient indigenous peoples of the Caucasus who have been living in the same place for many centuries. It would be fair to say that all of the societies of the North Caucasus have a very conservative culture. Among many peoples society is organized on the basis of tribes or clans known by a wide variety of terms, such as *tukhum, taipa* (*taip*), *qavum, jins, küp,* or *urugh* (*ru*).

(Interestingly, a number of these names are of Arabic origin.) There is also among some peoples a division of society into three classes: the "nobility," "freemen," and "slaves." There are widespread "avoidance customs" according to which couples are not supposed to be at their own wedding, show affection toward each other in public, or show any interest in their own children in the presence of their parents. Honor and chivalry are highly regarded. There is a distinctive culture of Caucasian music and dance, as well as an indigenous epic tradition (the ancient Nart sagas distantly related to other ancient Indo-European oral traditions). North Caucasians have also been famous for their martial prowess. There has been a curious mix among North Caucasians of proclaimed adherence to Islamic law (*shariat* in local languages) with a strong awareness of customary law governing traditional social behavior (*adat*).

Many of the peoples are Kipchak Turkic peoples. The Karachays and Balkars are two very closely related Kipchak Turkic peoples, though their origins might be distinct. They have many of the same features as other Kipchak Turkic peoples, including the custom of not marrying someone related within seven to nine generations along the father's line (though in some families this is not restricted to the father's line). There are traces of earlier Jewish and Christian influences in their language and culture, as well as strong influences from neighboring North Caucasian peoples. Like the other Kipchak Turkic peoples of the North Caucasus, the Karachays have a very strong tradition of consumption of dairy products such as yogurt, kefir, cheese, sour cream, and curds. Also very popular are lamb and other meats, including a traditional sausage made from liver (*jörme*). Wheat flour is used to make flatbread and especially fried or baked pies stuffed with cheese, potatoes, or greens. Fritters (*lokum*) are traditionally prepared for holidays. While the Kipchak Turks of the North Caucasus are Sunni Muslims, various pre-Islamic deities, beliefs, and rituals survived into the modern period.

One of the distinctive groups in the North Caucasians is the Adyge, a collective term for the Circassian and Ubykh peoples who live in the republics of Adygeya, Karachayevo-Cherkessia, and Kabardino-Balkaria. The western branch of the Circassian language is called Kyakh; the eastern branch, Kabarda. The Circassians traditionally practiced agriculture and animal husbandry. Their equivalent of a tribe was called the *tlapq*, and marriage was based on exogamy beyond the clan (but staying within the Adyge). The Circassians were actually divided into four classes or castes: princes, nobles, freemen, and slaves or vassals. The Circassians have a very highly developed sense of what constitutes proper conduct, and improper conduct was often met with vengeance, which explains the prevalence of blood feuds. While the Circassians have been predominantly Sunni Muslim for several hundred years or more, there appear to have been earlier Jewish and Christian influences—just as there are Jewish and Christian Circassians even today. The Nart sagas are a rich source for the earlier pagan gods of the Circassians, which have parallels in ancient India, Greece, and Scandinavia.

The Chechens and Ingush are two related peoples of the North Caucasus. In the highlands they raised animals, while in the lowlands they cultivated grain. Their traditional diet included both dairy products and grains, such as panbread stuffed with dairy or vegetables, and the Chechen version of *khingal* (a common culinary term in the North Caucasus), which was meat wrapped in dough boiled in a soup. Chechens have a form of social organization based on tribes (*taip*). Marriage is generally exogamous with respect to the clan but endogamous with respect to the tribe. In contrast to many other societies in the North Caucasus, traditional Chechen society is well known for being highly egalitarian. The only forms of hierarchy are based on age, kinship, and earned social honor. There is a strong code of etiquette, including a very strong principle of hospitality. A woman could bring dishonor upon her household and clan through immodest

DIVERSITY AMONG THE MUSLIMS IN RUSSIA			
Muslim People	**Population***	**Muslim People**	**Population***
Tatar	5,605,000	Nogay	91,000
Bashkir	1,674,000	Cherkes	61,000
Chechen	1,361,000	Abaza	38,000
Avar	757,000	Turkmen	33,000
Kazakh	655,000	Kyrgyz	32,000
Azerbaijani	621,000	Rutul	30,000
Kabarda	520,000	Agul	28,000
Dargin	510,000	Abkhaz	11,000
Kumyk	423,000	Arab	11,000
Ingush	412,000	Tsakhur	10,000
Lezgin	412,000	Crimean Tatar	4,000
Karachay	192,000	Persian	4,000
Lak	156,000	Shapsug	3,000
Tabasaran	132,000	Uygur	3,000
Adyge	129,000	Karakalpak	2,000
Uzbek	123,000	Dungan	1,000
Tajik	120,000	Adjar	300
Balkar	108,000	Arab (Centr. Asian)	200
Turk	95,000		
TOTAL	**12,491,000**		

*Note: Population figures are from the 2002 Russian census.

behavior (including being raped). Traces of past contacts with the Georgian church can still be discerned, but the Chechens have been Sunni Muslim for the past several centuries. Earlier they practiced an animistic religion that featured a number of deities, a cult of ancestors, and belief in an afterlife. Funerary rites included burial the day after death and additional feasts several days later, two years later, and three years later.

Finally, Dagestan is a land of many different peoples. The largest group, the Avars, number some 757,000 and make up about one-fifth of the population of the republic. Other important peoples include the Dargins (510,000), Kumyks (423,000), Lezgins (412,000), Laks (156,000), Tabasarans (132,000), and Nogays (91,000). The Kumyks and Nogays are Kipchak Turkic peoples. The Kumyks are similar to the Karachay-Balkars, but since they live in the valleys they have come under greater influence from their neighbors in terms of their culture (for example, their foodways) and their language. The Nogays are very closely related to the Kazakhs in language, though their culture shows some strong Caucasian influences. Like the Kazakhs, they were nomads until the time of the Bolshevik Revolution. (In Central Asia, Kazan Tatars are known as "Nogay.")

The remaining peoples of Dagestan are ancient indigenous peoples. While most of the other groups refer to clans as *tukhum*, the Avars, for whom the concept is very strong, use the word *tlibil*. In contrast to many other groups, the Avars have a tradition of endogamy and may marry first cousins. The Avars are also unlike many other peoples of the North Caucasus in that they live in nuclear families. However, like many other peoples of the North Caucasus, Avars have a three-tiered class system comprising aristocrats, freedmen, and slaves. In traditional society there was a twofold system of judges, one system based on customary law and another based on Islamic religious law. The Islam practiced by the Dargins, Lezgins, and other peoples of Dagestan is considered to include many aspects of the region's pre-Islamic belief system.

A muezzin issues the call to prayer from the minaret of a mosque in Russia. The future of Islam in Russian society remains unclear.

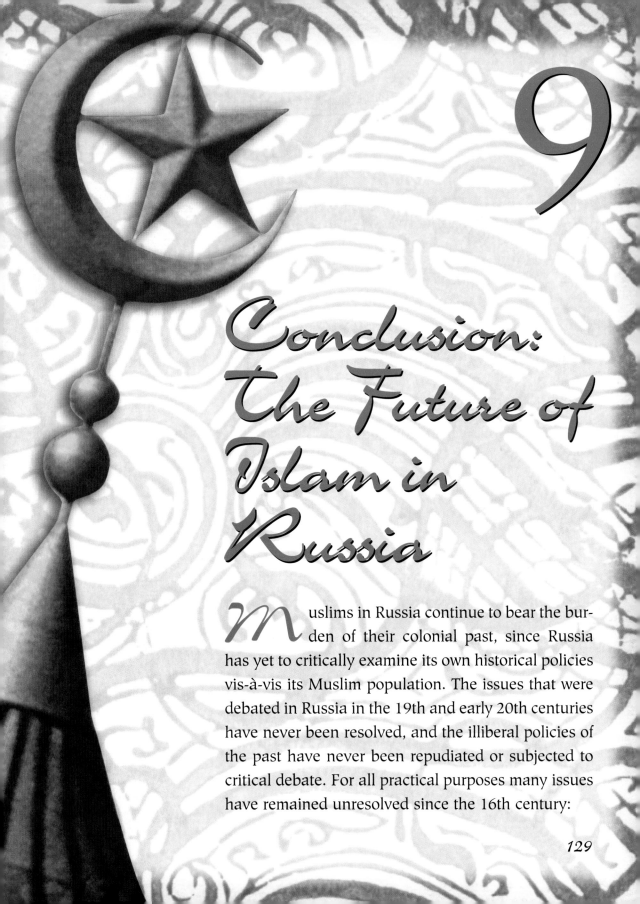

9

Conclusion: The Future of Islam in Russia

Muslims in Russia continue to bear the burden of their colonial past, since Russia has yet to critically examine its own historical policies vis-à-vis its Muslim population. The issues that were debated in Russia in the 19th and early 20th centuries have never been resolved, and the illiberal policies of the past have never been repudiated or subjected to critical debate. For all practical purposes many issues have remained unresolved since the 16th century:

- Should Orthodox Christianity and Russian culture be the official religion and culture of the state, or is Russia a multi-confessional, multi-ethnic state?

- Should Russia's minorities be pressured to assimilate to the dominant religion, or should the state protect and promote the religious faiths of its minorities?

- Should Russia's minorities be pressured to assimilate to the dominant culture, or should the state protect and promote the culture of its minorities?

- Should the state (and society) regard the liberal Islam of its citizens as an asset, or should it continue to see all Muslims as a threat, echoing the views of 19th- and 20th-century colonialist ideology?

These days, the Muslims of the Russian Federation (and the other successor states to the USSR) have the burden of demonstrating that they are not "fanatics" or a "threat."

Misunderstandings and Missteps

The post-Soviet renaissance in Islamic belief and practice has led to serious misunderstandings among Russian policymakers and the Russian public alike. Countless misleading statements have appeared in the Russian media concerning the role of Islam in the Volga region, for example. In a 1994 interview, President Shaymiyev of Tatarstan was asked about the threat to Russia from Islamic fundamentalism, which the interviewer postulated would arrive from Asia via Tatarstan and Bashqortostan. In describing this supposed threat, the interviewer even used the term *fifth column* to characterize Muslims in Russia. President Shaymiyev responded that there was no threat of Islamic fundamentalism in Tatarstan. Islam and Christianity, he observed, were the two faiths of Tatarstan, and relations between these two religions had been problem free for many years. He also noted that while some countries might be interested in propagating fundamentalism, Tatarstan was looking to more enlightened countries. On the other hand, Shaymiyev stated that in the future the Muslim voice in Russian politics would be heard, even though it was not heard in the case of Russia's policy toward the Muslims of Bosnia. Seen from this perspective, concerns about Islamic fundamentalism in the Volga region seem to represent at best a sad misunderstanding of the region's pre-Soviet culture.

The situation is quite different in the North Caucasus. Rather than choosing the path of negotiation, in both 1994 and 1999 the Russian government took the path of armed suppression of the Chechen people. To anyone outside the Russian government, the results have been predictable. The conflict in Chechnya is a human rights tragedy of the first order, and the behavior of the Russian military has raised international consternation. Rather than defusing the situation in Chechnya, the Russian government's policies since 1991 have served only to steadily radicalize the population, attract Islamist fighters who formerly fought in Afghanistan, and turn the North Caucasus into a growing bastion of Wahhabism. The situation in the North Caucasus needs to be resolved before the conflict spreads beyond the boundaries of Chechnya and before the Chechen people are completely dispersed for the second time in six decades. The more the state oppresses its citizens, the more they resort to violence, as has been seen in Moscow and Beslan. In addition, continued ill treatment of North Caucasian refugees, particularly in Moscow, threatens to make ethnic violence a fact of life in that city, too.

In comparing Russia's post-1991 policies vis-à-vis its religious and ethnic minorities with the earlier imperial policies, it is difficult to see a tremendous qualitative difference. There are still many Russian projects or policies that, in practice if not necessarily by design, might have the effect of assimilating ethnic and religious minorities. It is not clear, however, to

Vladimir Putin can be seen on a large screen as he addresses the opening session of the Organization of the Islamic Conference (OIC) summit in Malaysia, October 2003. The OIC includes more than 55 nations with predominantly Muslim populations. In 2005 Russia was granted the status of observer to the OIC, giving it a limited role in the organization. Russian leaders hoped this would help foster closer ties with Muslim countries, in addition to better relations with Russian Muslims in Chechnya and elsewhere.

what extent—if at all—there might be pressure for Muslims to convert to Orthodox Christianity. The fact that the government has declared Russian Orthodox Christianity, Buddhism, and Islam as the three traditional faiths of Russia demonstrates that there is an awareness of the role of Islam in Russia's history. At the same time, the Russian government is not a monolith. Unexpected controversies continue over symbolic issues relating to religion, such as the ban on Muslim women wearing headscarves in their official passport photographs (overturned by a successful court appeal in May 2003). Proposals have been introduced to include lessons on Orthodox Christianity in Russian classrooms; there is disagreement over whether these would be optional or required. Would such lessons, Muslims ask, be replaced by lessons on Islam in classrooms in Tatarstan (or in other areas with high concentrations of Tatars and other Muslims)? Muslims complain that most official state functions and ceremonies include Russian Orthodox priests, but usually exclude Muslim clerics. Specialists have even floated the idea of a Russian government project for creating a "Russian Islam"—which is in effect a proposal to use Islam as a basis for assimilating Russia's ethnic minorities. They would retain their faith, but they would Russianize linguistically and culturally.

Finally, the occasional calls by Russian politicians to eliminate the ethnic republics, if ever realized, might well have serious unintended consequences, including the further radicalization of Muslim peoples of the Russian Federation. Denying these peoples the possibility of continuing the institutionalized existence of their national language and culture would only serve to increase the religious component of their identity. If as a next step the state sought to suppress Islam, it would only succeed in driving it underground. As is known from other parts of the Muslim world, underground religious networks form the infrastructure for resistance to authoritarian states and are the most difficult to control. Were it to follow such a policy, the Russian Federation would likely succeed only in creating far greater problems for itself.

Arguably the best course of action for the Russian Federation would be to return to the idea of federalism and to recognize that a multi-confessional, multi-ethnic state can be a source of strength. As Ismail Bey Gaspirali would have said, Russia's Muslims can be good citizens.

anathema—something that is intensely disliked.

apostasy—the renunciation of one's religious faith.

caliphate—the Islamic political empire, which was presided over by a ruler known as a caliph (considered a successor to Muhammad as the spiritual and temporal head of Islam).

Chinggisid—of or relating to one of the descendants of the Mongol conqueror Chinggis Khan (Genghis Khan).

diaspora—a community of people living away from their ancestral homeland.

exogamy—the practice of marrying outside of one's group, especially when required by custom or law.

hajj—the pilgrimage to Mecca, which all Muslims who are able are obligated to make at least once in their lifetime.

imam—a Muslim prayer leader or head of a mosque.

khanate—the dominion or state ruled by a khan.

madrasa—an Islamic religious school.

mufti—a Muslim scholar or jurist who interprets Islamic law by issuing a ruling known as a *fatwa*.

muftiate—the jurisdiction presided over by a mufti.

patrimony—lands or an estate inherited from one's father.

Sharia—Islamic religious law.

shaykh—a Muslim religious teacher, especially a Sufi master; a chieftain or elder.

Glossary

Sufi orders—any of various communities, typically following a particular spiritual teacher or master, in the Islamic mystical tradition of Sufism.

Sufism—Islamic mysticism.

Wahhabism—a puritanical form of Islam, founded by the 18th-century reformer Muhammad ibn Abd al-Wahhab and dominant today in Saudi Arabia, that advocates purging Islam of all "un-Islamic" influences, including Shia and Sufi practices.

Zoroastrianism—a religion (originating in Persia probably around the sixth century B.C.) holding that Ahura Mazda, the supreme god, is locked in a struggle against the evil spirit Ahriman, and that the good deeds of humans assist Ahura Mazda in this cosmic contest.

Allworth, E., ed. *Central Asia: 130 Years of Russian Dominance, A Historical Overview*. Durham, N.C.: Duke University Press, 1994.

———. ed. *Tatars of the Crimea: Their Struggle for Survival*. Durham, N.C.: Duke University Press, 1988.

Bennigsen, Alexandre, and S. Enders Wimbush. *Mystics and Commissars. Muslims of the Soviet Empire, A Guide*. Bloomington: Indiana University Press, 1985.

Brower, Daniel R., and Edward J. Lazzerini, eds. *Russia's Orient: Imperial Borderlands and Peoples, 1700–1917*. Indiana-Michigan Series in Russian and East European Studies. Bloomington: Indiana University Press, 1997.

Bukharaev, Ravil. *Islam in Russia: The Four Seasons*. Richmond, UK: Curzon, 2000.

———. *The Model of Tatarstan Under President Mintimer Shaimiev*. Richmond, UK: Curzon, 1999.

Chenciner, Robert. *Daghestan: Tradition and Survival*. New York: Palgrave Macmillan, 1997.

Colarusso, John. *Nart Sagas from the Caucasus: Myths and Legends from the Circassians, Abazas, Abkhaz, and Ubykhs*. Princeton, N.J.: Princeton University Press, 2002.

DeWeese, Devin. *Islamization and Native Religion in the Golden Horde: Baba Tükles and Conversion to Islam in Historical and Epic Tradition*. University Park: The Pennsylvania State University Press, 1994.

Edgar, Adrienne Lynn. *Tribal Nation: The Making of Soviet Turkmenistan*. Princeton, N.J.: Princeton University Press, 2004.

Findley, Carter Vaughn. *The Turks in World History*. Oxford: Oxford University Press, 2004.

Selected Bibliography

Fisher, Alan W. *The Crimean Tatars*. Stanford, Calif.: Hoover Institution Press, 1978.

Foltz, Richard C. *Religions of the Silk Road: Overland Trade and Cultural Exchange from Antiquity to the Fifteenth Century*. New York: St. Martin's, 1999.

Frye, Richard N. *The Heritage of Central Asia from Antiquity to the Turkish Expansion*. Princeton, N.J.: Markus Wiener Publishers, 1996.

Gammer, Moshe. *Muslim Resistance to the Tsar: Shamil and the Conquest of Chechnia and Daghestan*. London: Frank Cass, 1994.

Gasprinskii, Ismail. "Russo-Oriental Relations: Thoughts, Notes, and Desires," Translated by Edward J. Lazzerini. In *Tatars of the Crimea: Their Struggle for Survival*, edited by Edward Allworth, 202–216. Durham, N.C.: Duke University Press, 1988.

Geraci, Robert P. *Windows on the East: National and Imperial Identities in Late Tsarist Russia*. Ithaca, N.Y.: Cornell University Press, 2001.

Geraci, Robert P., and Michael Khodarkovsky, eds. *Of Religion and Empire: Missions, Conversion, and Tolerance in Tsarist Russia*. Ithaca, N.Y.: Cornell University Press, 2001.

Gross, Jo-Ann, ed. *Muslims in Central Asia: Expressions of Identity and Change*. Durham, N.C.: Duke University Press, 1992.

de Hartog, L. *Russia and the Mongol Yoke: The History of the Russian Principalities and the Golden Horde, 1221–1502*. London: British Academic Press, 1996.

Hewitt, George, ed. *The Abkhazians: A Handbook*. New York: Palgrave Macmillan, 1998.

Hirsch, Francine. *Empire of Nations: Ethnographic Knowledge and the Making of the Soviet Union*. Ithaca, N.Y.: Cornell University Press, 2005.

Hopkirk, Peter. *The Great Game: The Struggle for Empire in Central Asia*. New York: Kodansha International, 1994.

Jaimoukha, Amjad. *The Chechens: A Handbook*. New York: RoutledgeCurzon, 2005.

———. *The Circassians: A Handbook*. Richmond, UK: Curzon, 2001.

Kappeler, Andreas. *The Russian Empire: A Multiethnic History*. Translated by Alfred Clayton. Harlow, UK: Longman, 2001.

Keller, Shoshona. *To Moscow, Not Mecca: The Soviet Campaign Against Islam in Central Asia, 1917–1941*. Westport, Conn.: Praeger, 2001.

Kendirbay, Gulnar. "The National Liberation Movement of the Kazakh Intelligentsia at the Beginning of the 20th Century." *Central Asian Survey* 16, no. 4 (1997): 487–516.

Khalid, Adeeb. *The Politics of Muslim Cultural Reform: Jadidism in Central Asia*. Berkeley: University of California Press, 1998.

Khazanov, Anatoly M. *After the USSR: Ethnicity, Nationalism and Politics in the Commonwealth of Independent States*. Madison: University of Wisconsin Press, 1995.

Khodarkovsky, Michael. *Russia's Steppe Frontier: The Making of a Colonial Empire, 1500–1800*. Bloomington: Indiana University Press, 2002.

Manz, B. F. *The Rise and Rule of Tamerlane*. Cambridge Studies in Islamic Civilization. Cambridge: Cambridge University Press, 1989.

Manz, Beatrice F., ed. *Central Asia in Historical Perspective*. Boulder, Colo.: Westview Press, 1994.

Selected Bibliography

Martin, Virginia. *Law and Custom in the Steppe: The Kazakhs of the Middle Horde and Russian Colonialism in the Nineteenth Century.* Richmond, UK: Curzon, 2002.

McChesney, Robert D. *Central Asia: Foundations of Change.* Princeton, N.J.: The Darwin Press, 1996.

———. *Waqf in Central Asia: Four Hundred Years in the History of a Muslim Shrine, 1480–1889.* Princeton, N.J.: Princeton University Press, 1991.

Northrop, Douglas. *Veiled Empire: Gender and Power in Stalinist Central Asia.* Ithaca, N.Y.: Cornell University Press, 2004.

Olcott, Martha Brill. *The Kazakhs.* Stanford, Calif.: Hoover Institution Press, 1995.

Ostrowski, Donald. *The Mongols and Russia.* Cambridge: Cambridge University Press, 1998.

Paksoy, H.B., ed. *Central Asia Reader: The Rediscovery of History.* Armonk, N.Y.: M.E. Sharpe, 1996.

Pilkington, H., and G. Yemelianova, eds. *Private and Public Faces of Islam in Post-Soviet Russia.* London: RoutledgeCurzon, 2002.

Rabghuzi. *The Stories of the Prophets: Qisas al-anbiya', An Eastern Turkish Version.* Edited and translated by H. E. Boeschoten et al. Leiden: Brill, 1995.

Rashid, Ahmed. *Jihad: The Rise of Militant Islam in Central Asia.* New Haven, Conn.: Yale University Press, 2002.

———. *Taliban: Militant Islam, Oil & Fundamentalism in Central Asia.* New Haven, Conn.: Yale University Press, 2001.

Rorlich, Azade-Ayse. *The Volga Tatars: A Profile in National Resilience.* Stanford, Calif.: Hoover Institution Press, 1986.

Roy, Olivier. *The New Central Asia: The Creation of Nations.* New York: New York University Press, 2000.

Schamiloglu, Uli. "The Formation of a Tatar Historical Consciousness: Sihabäddin Märcani and The Image of the Golden Horde." *Central Asian Survey* 9, no. 2 (1990): 39–49.

———. *The Golden Horde: Economy, Society, and Civilization in Western Eurasia, Thirteenth-Fourteenth Centuries.* Madison, Wis.: Turko-Tatar Press, in press.

———. "Ictihad or Millat?: Reflections on Bukhara, Kazan, and the Legacy of Russian Orientalism." In *Reform Movements and Revolutions in Turkistan: 1900–1924.* Studies in Honour of Osman Khoja, edited by Timur Kocaoglu, 347–368. Haarlem, The Netherlands: SOTA, 2001.

———. "The Islamic High Culture of the Golden Horde." *Proceedings of the 2nd Symposium on Islam in the Volga-Ural Region.* Istanbul: Research Center for Islamic History, Art and Culture, in press.

———. "Preliminary Remarks on the Role of Disease in the History of the Golden Horde." *Central Asian Survey* 12, no. 4 (1993): 447–457.

———. "The Rise of the Ottoman Empire: The Black Death in Medieval Anatolia and its Impact on Turkish Civilization." In *Views from the Edge: Essays in Honor of Richard W. Bulliet,* edited by Neguin Yavari, Lawrence G. Potter, and Jean-Marc Oppenheim, 255–279. New York: Columbia University Press, 2004.

———. "We Are Not Tatars! The Invention of a Bulgar Identity." In *Néptörténet – Nyelvtörténet. A 70 éves Róna-Tas András köszöntése,* edited by László Károly and Éva Nagy Kincses, 137–153. Szeged: 2001.

Selected Bibliography

Schimmel, Annemarie. *Mystical Dimensions of Islam*. Chapel Hill: University of North Carolina Press, 1975.

Soucek, Svat. *A History of Inner Asia*. Cambridge: Cambridge University Press, 2000.

Swietochowski, Tadeusz. *Russia and Azerbaijan: A Borderland in Transition*. New York: Columbia University Press, 1995.

———. *Russian Azerbaijan, 1905–1920: The Shaping of a National Identity in a Muslim Community*. Cambridge: Cambridge University Press, 1985.

Whitfield, Susan. *Life Along the Silk Road*. Berkeley: University of California Press, 2000.

Williams, Brian Glyn. *The Crimean Tatars: The Diaspora Experience and the Forging of Nation*. Leiden: E. J. Brill, 2001.

Yemelianova, Galina. "Islam and Nation-Building in Tatarstan and Dagestan of the Russian Federation." *Nationalities Papers* 27, no. 4 (1999): 605–630.

———. "The National Identity of the Volga Tatars at the Turn of the 19th Century: Tatarism, Turkism and Islam." *Central Asian Survey* 16, no. 4 (1997): 543–572.

———. "Sufism and Politics in the North Caucasus." *Nationalities Papers* 29, no. 4 (2001): 661–688.

Zelkina, Anna. *In Quest for God and Freedom: Sufi Responses to the Russian Advance in the North Caucasus*. New York: New York University Press, 2000.

Zenkovsky, Serge A. *Pan-Turkism and Islam in Russia*. Cambridge, Mass.: Harvard University Press, 1960.

http://www.jamestown.org/

The Jamestown Foundation has a number of on-line publications, including the *Eurasia Daily Monitor, Global Terrorism Analysis*, and *Chechnya Weekly*.

http://www.cacianalyst.org/

The *Central Asia-Caucasus Analyst* is published by the Central Asia-Caucasus Institute of the School of Advanced International Studies, The Johns Hopkins University.

http://www.csis.org/

The Center for Strategic and International Studies has an Islamic Studies Program with a new project on "Islam in Russia."

http://eng.islam.ru/

Islam.ru is an independent Islamic information channel in Russia. This English-language site includes news and analysis, interviews, and articles on various aspects of Islam.

http://www.kafkas.org.tr/english/

The Turkey-based Caucasus Foundation offers various pages on the culture and history of the Caucasus.

http://www.tatar.net/

This page collects links relating to the Crimean Tatars.

http://www.iccrimea.org/

The International Committee for Crimea is a rich source of information on the Crimean Tatars. The page entitled "Celebrating the Life of Ismail Bey Gaspirali" includes a range of scholarly articles on this important figure.

Internet Resources

http://www.eurasianet.org/

Eurasianet.org is a comprehensive source for news and information about the countries of the Caucasus and Central Asia (excluding Russia).

http://kcr.narod.ru/karachay.html

The official website of the Karachay-Cherkess Republic, with links to additional websites, such as the Karachay-Malkar home page.

http://www.kcn.ru/tat_en/index.htm

Tatarstan on the Internet, including links to the official website of the Republic of Tatarstan, the city of Kazan, and Kazan State University.

http://www.bashedu.ru/bashkortostan/bash_e.htm

Bashqortostan on the Internet.

Abilay Khan, 58
Afghanistan, 91–92
agriculture, 24, 26, *59*, 118–119, 125
Ahrar, Khoja Ubaydullah, 51
Ahundzade, Mirza Fäth Äli, 68
Aitmatov, Chingis, 89
All-Russian Congress of Muslims, 73–75
   See also Muslims
Altinsarin, Ibray, 62, 69
Andropov, Yuri, 90
atheism, 81–82
   See also Spiritual Boards; USSR (Union
   of Soviet Socialist Republics)

Bakharzi, Shaykh Sayf ad-Din, 44
Basayev, Shamil, 110
Bashqortostan, 18, 97, 100, 116
Batu (Khan), 43, 54
Bennigsen, Alexandre, 85
Berke Khan, 44
al-Biruni, *36*, 37
Black Death. *See* bubonic plague
Bolshevik Revolution (1917), 13, 77–78
   See also USSR (Union of Soviet
   Socialist Republics)
Boraq Khan, 42
Brezhnev, Leonid, 90
bubonic plague, 32, 46–47, 51, 53
Bukhara, 34, 35, 36, 42, 61, 66
Bukhari, 35
al-Bulghari, Abdärrähim Utiz Imäni, 66

Catherine the Great, 55–56, 61
Caucasus (geographic region), 24
Central Spiritual Board of Russia and the
   CIS, 103–104
   See also Spiritual Boards
Chaghatay Khanate, 42, 46–47, 49–50
   See also medieval history
Chechnya, 19, 21, 29, 105, 108–113, 131

Chernenko, Konstantin, 90
Chinggis Khan (Genghis Khan), 41–43, 53
   See also Golden Horde
climate, 24
Commonwealth of Independent States
   (CIS), 95
   See also Russian Federation
conversion, religious
   from Christianity to Islam, 21
   from Islam to Christianity, 54–55,
     60–61, 62, 132
   and Islamization, 39–40, 44
culture
   education, 62, 66–68, 70, 82–83,
     85–87, 98–100, 107
   and family life, 119–120, 124, 125, 127
   and Islamization, 39–40, 44, 61–62
   literature, 35, 36–37, 44–46, 47, 61–62,
     68–71, 87–89
   and Muslim nationality, 82, 83–87,
     89–90
   See also ethnic groups

Dagestan, 33, 56, 57, 98–99, 110,
   126–127
Derbent (present-day Dagestan), 33, 34,
   56
Dudayev, Dzhokhar, 108–109

education, 62, 82–83, 85–87, 98–100, 107
   and Islamic modernism, 66–68, 70
ethnic groups
   Bashkirs, 18, 116–120
   and conflict in the Russian Empire, 57
   and culture, 115–127
   Kazakhs, 19, 58–59, 75, 121–123
   as minorities, 21, 29, 112–113, 130
   in the North Caucasus, 123–127
   organization of, in the USSR, 13–14
   populations of, 96, *126*, 127

Numbers in **bold italic** refer to captions.

Index

Tatars, 18–19, 60–61, 62, 69, 71–72, 74–75, 79, 83, 92, 105–108, 116–121
See also regions

family life, 119–120, 124, 125, 127
Firdawsi, 35
five pillars (of Islam), 15–16
See also Islam
foreign aid, 101, *102*, 103–104

Gainutdin, Ravil, 103
Gaspirali, Ismail (Ismail Gasprinsky), 70–71, 133
Genghis Khan. *See* Chinggis Khan (Genghis Khan)
geographic features, 23–26
See also regions
Golden Horde, 42–47, 49–51
collapse of the, 52–54
See also medieval history
Gorbachev, Mikhail, 90–93
Gülen, Fethullah, 99

Hajib, Yusuf Khass, 37

Ibn Battuta, 44, 61
Ibn Fadlan, 37–38, 117
Ibn Sina, 36–37
Il'minskii, Nikolai I., 62
Iskhaki, Ayaz, 69
Islam
All-Russian Congress of Muslims, 73–75
caliphate (spread of), 31–39
description of, 14–15
five pillars of, 15–16
future of, in the Russian Federation, 20–21, 129–133
holidays of, 120, 123
and Islamization, 39–40, 44, 61–62
legal schools in, 16
and modernism, 65–72
Sufism, 40, 44, *45*, 51, 52, 57, 61–62,

85, 102, 110, 120–121
Sunni and Shia schism in, 16–17
Wahhabism, 99, 100, 101–102, 110, 121
See also conversion, religious; Muslims
Ivan the Terrible (Ivan IV), 53, 56

Jadidism, 70
Jami, 51
Jöchi (Khan), 42–43

Kadyrov, Akhmad, 110, 111
Karakhanid dynasty, 35–36
See also medieval history
Kashgari, Mahmud, 37
Kasyanov, Mikhail, *102*
Kazakh hordes, 58
Khanate of Kazan, 13, *20*, 27, 52–54
See also Russian Empire
Khanate of Khiva, 58, 60
khanates, 52–53
Russian Empire expansion into, 56–61
See also Russian Empire
Khazar state, 33–34, 37
See also medieval history
Khrushchev, Nikita, 89
al-Khwarezmi, 37
al-Khwarezmi, Muhammad ibn Muhammad ibn Khusrev, 45–46
Kök Türk Empire, 32–33
Kolbin, Gennadii, 92
Kunayev, Dinmukhamed, 92

land area, 23
languages, 19, 35, 71, 116–117, 123, 125
and education, 62, 82–83, 86–87, 90
and scripts, 47, 68, 86–87, 108
Lenin, Vladimir, 77–78, 88
literature, 35, 36–37, 44–46, 47, 68–71, 87–89
and Sufism, 61–62

Märjani, Shihabäddin, 66–68, 70, 71–72

Maskhadov, Aslan, 109, 110, 111, *112*
medieval history
   and the bubonic plague, 46–47, 49
   and Islamization, 39–40
   Karakhanid dynasty, 35–36
   Khazar state, 33–34, 37
   Kök Türk Empire, 32–33
   and the Mongol Empire, 41–46
   Samanid state, 35
   and spread of Islam to Russia, 31–33
   Volga Bulgarian state, 37–38
Melikov-Zarbadi, Hasan, 68
modernism, Islamic, 65–72
Mongol Empire, 41–46
   See also Golden Horde
Moscow, 26–27, 53, 116
mosques, 97, 100
Muhammad, 14–15, 16, 17, 31, 35
   See also Islam
ibn Muslim, Qutayba, 34–35
Muslims
   persecution of, in the Russian
     Federation, 112–113
   persecution of, in the USSR, 28–29, 81,
     83–90
   population of, in the Russian
     Federation, *12*, 14, 96, *126*, 127
   population of, in the USSR, 13–14
   regional populations of, 26, 29
   in the Russian Empire, 54–56, 60–63,
     73–75
   in the Russian Federation, 96–101
   See also Islam
Muslims of the Russian Federation, 101

Najibullah, Mohammed, *91*
Nasiri, Qayyum, 69
nationalism, 71–72, 75, 81–82, 89–90,
   92–93, 112
   in the Russian Federation, 104–105
   See also regions
Navai, Ali Shir, 50
Nicholas II (Tsar), 74, 77

"October Revolution." *See* Bolshevik
   Revolution (1917)
Orda (Khan), 43
Organization of the Islamic Conference
   (OIC), *132*
Özbek Khan (Uzbek), 44, 51

Peter the Great (Tsar), 54, 56
political organization
   in the Russian Empire, 73–75
   in the USSR, 79–81
population
   Muslim, in the Russian Federation, *12*,
     14, 96, 116, *126*, 127
   Muslim, in the USSR, 13–14
Putin, Vladimir, 96, *104*, 106–107, 111,
   113, *132*

Qunanbay, Abay, 69
Qur'an, 15, 16, *38*, 66–68
   See also Islam
Qursavi, Abdännasir, 66, *67*

Rashid, Ahmed, 85
reform, Islamic. *See* modernism, Islamic
regions
   Central Asia, 17, 26, 38, 58, 60, 69–70,
     79–80, 122–123
   Crimea, 24, 26, 38, 43, 44, 72
   Middle Volga, 17–19, 26–27, 38, 43,
     61–62, 69, 71–72, 75, 79, 116
   and Muslim populations, 26
   North Caucasus, 17, 19, 24, 26, 38, 57,
     81, 100–101, 112, 116, 123–126
   political, in the USSR, 79–81
   and religious officials, 100–101
   Siberia, 25, 26, 39, 121
   South Caucasus, 17, 24, 26, 38, 56–57,
     80, 101, 116
religion
   Orthodox Christianity, 21, 60–62, 97,
     132–133
   and the Russian Federation, 20–21,

Index

100–105, 129–132
See also Islam
republics
  in the Russian Federation, 17, 21, 29,
    97, 100–101, 104–113
  in the USSR (Union of Soviet Socialist
    Republics), 13–14, 28–29, 79–81
Rudaki, 35
Russian Empire, 13, 26–28
  expansion of the, 56–61
  and Islamic modernism, 65–72
  and the Khanate of Kazan, 53–54
  and the persecution of Muslims, 54–56,
    60–63
  rise of political movements in the,
    73–75
  See also Russian Federation; USSR
    (Union of Soviet Socialist Republics)
Russian Federation
  climate, 24
  and ethnic groups, 17–19, 21, 29,
    112–113
  future of Islam in the, 20–21, 129–133
  geographic features, 23–26
  and independent states, 14, 17, 26, 93,
    95–97
  land area and borders, 23, 26–27
  Muslim population in, *12*, 14, 96, 116,
    126, 127
  and religion, 20–21, 100–105
  republics of the, 17, 21, 29, 97,
    100–101, 104–113
  See also Russian Empire; USSR (Union
    of Soviet Socialist Republics)
Russian Islamic University, 99

Samarkand, 34, 35, 42, *48*, 50, 61
Satuk Bughra Khan, 35
scripts. *See* languages
Shamil, Imam, 57–58
Shaybanids, 50–51
  See also Golden Horde
Shaykh Muhammad Arif North Caucasian

Islamic University, 98
Shaymiyev (President of Tatarstan), 109
ibn Shilki, Almush, 37
Soviet Union. *See* USSR (Union of Soviet
  Socialist Republics)
Spiritual Boards, 84–86, 103
St. Petersburg, *25*, 26, 77, 116
Stalin, Joseph, 28–29, 78, 81, 88, 90
steppe zone, 24–25, 26
"Stories of the Prophets" (*Qisas ül-
  enbiya'*), 44–45
  See also literature
Sufism, 40, 44, *45*, 51, 52, 57, 61–62, 85,
  102, 110, 120–121
  See also Islam
Suleymenov, Olzhas, 92
Sultangaliev, Mirsaid, 83
Sunni and Shia schism, 16–17
  See also Islam

Tajetdin, Talgat, 103, *104*
Tamerlane (Timur the Lame), *48*, 49–51
Tarmashirin, 42
Tatarstan, 18, 28, 97, 100, 105–109, 113,
  130–131
Tinibek Khan, 45
Töde Mengü Khan, 44
trade, 43, 50, 55, 121

Ushurma, Mansur, 57
USSR (Union of Soviet Socialist
  Republics)
  atheism policy of the, 81–82
  collapse of the, 14, 20, 28–29, 92–93,
    95, 105
  and culture, 87–89
  formation of the, 77–78
  and "friendship of peoples" ideology,
    28–29
  under Mikhail Gorbachev, 90–93
  and Muslim culture, 81, 83–89
  "nationalities problem," 90–92
  republics in, 13–14, 28–29, 79–81

Spiritual Boards, 84–86, 103
See also Russian Empire; Russian
 Federation

Valikhanov, Chokan, 59
Volga River, 25–26, *27*

Wahhabism, 99, 100, 101–102, 110, 121

Wimbush, S. Enders, 85
World War II, 88–89

Yeltsin, Boris, 93, 95–96, 109

Zhangir Khan, 58
Zoroastrianism, 34, 39, *40*, 123

Picture Credits

The **FOREIGN POLICY RESEARCH INSTITUTE (FPRI)** served as editorial consultants for the GROWTH AND INFLUENCE OF ISLAM IN THE NATIONS OF ASIA AND CENTRAL ASIA series. FPRI is one of the nation's oldest "think tanks." The Institute's Middle East Program focuses on Gulf security, monitors the Arab-Israeli peace process, and sponsors an annual conference for teachers on the Middle East, plus periodic briefings on key developments in the region.

Among the FPRI's trustees is a former Secretary of State and a former Secretary of the Navy (and among the FPRI's former trustees and interns, two current Undersecretaries of Defense), not to mention two university presidents emeritus, a foundation president, and several active or retired corporate CEOs.

The scholars of FPRI include a former aide to three U.S. Secretaries of State, a Pulitzer Prize–winning historian, a former president of Swarthmore College and a Bancroft Prize–winning historian, and two former staff members of the National Security Council. And the FPRI counts among its extended network of scholars— especially its Inter-University Study Groups—representatives of diverse disciplines, including political science, history, economics, law, management, religion, sociology, and psychology.

DR. HARVEY SICHERMAN is president and director of the Foreign Policy Research Institute in Philadelphia, Pennsylvania. He has extensive experience in writing, research, and analysis of U.S. foreign and national security policy, both in government and out. He served as Special Assistant to Secretary of State Alexander M. Haig Jr. and as a member of the Policy Planning Staff of Secretary of State James A. Baker III. Dr. Sicherman was also a consultant to Secretary of the Navy John F. Lehman Jr. (1982–1987) and Secretary of State George Shultz (1988).

A graduate of the University of Scranton (B.S., History, 1966), Dr. Sicherman earned his Ph.D. at the University of Pennsylvania (Political Science, 1971), where he received a Salvatori Fellowship. He is author or editor of numerous books and articles, including *America the Vulnerable: Our Military Problems and How to Fix Them* (FPRI, 2002) and *Palestinian Autonomy, Self-Government and Peace* (Westview Press, 1993). He edits *Peacefacts*, an FPRI bulletin that monitors the Arab-Israeli peace process.

ULI SCHAMILOGLU received a B.A. in Middle East Languages and Cultures from Columbia College and M.A., M.Phil., and Ph.D. degrees in History from Columbia University. Since 1989 he has been teaching at the University of Wisconsin-Madison, where he is Professor of Turkic & Central Eurasian Studies in the Department of Languages and Cultures of Asia. He also serves as chair of the Central Asian Studies Program and associate director of the Center for Middle East Studies at the University of Wisconsin-Madison. He is the author of numerous articles on the socioeconomic history of medieval Eurasia and the modern intellectual history of the Muslims of the Russian Empire. He is also the author of *The Golden Horde: Economy, Society, and Civilization in Western Eurasia, Thirteenth-Fourteenth Centuries* (in press); a translation of the "Clear Path to Heaven" (a 14th-century Turkic manual of Islam from the Golden Horde, in progress); and *Turkic and Tatar Thought in the Liberal Age* (forthcoming).